THE MONK
AND THE
RIDDLE

The Monk and the Riddle

The Education of a Silicon Valley Entrepreneur

Randy Komisar
with Kent Lineback

Harvard Business School Press
Boston, Massachusetts

The Web sites or URLs mentioned in this book originated in my imagi-
nation. Some of them may coincide with the names or URLs of real
sites. This is fortuitous, and no resemblance should be inferred. All ref-
erences to my life — personal and professional — are based in fact, but
they reflect my interpretation of events. Lenny, Allison, and Frank are
composite portraits of would-be entrepreneurs and venture capitalists
with whom I interact daily. Their characters and their dialogue, however
fictionalized, are true to my experiences.

Library of Congress Cataloging-in-Publication Data

Komisar, Randy, 1954–
    The monk and the riddle : the education of a Silicon Valley entrepreneur / Randy
    Komisar, with Kent Lineback.
        p. cm.
    Includes index.
    ISBN 1-57851-140-2 (alk. paper)
    1. Komisar, Randy, 1954–   2. Businesspeople–United States–Biography.   3.
Entrepreneurship–United States–Biography.   I. Lineback, Kent L.   II. Title.

HC102.5.K66 A3 2000
338'.04'092–dc21
[B]   99-057378

The paper used in this publication meets the requirements of the
American National Standard for Permanence of Paper for Publications
and Documents in Libraries and Archives Z39.48-1992.

For D2 and T2

Every moment some form grows perfect in hand or face; some tone on the hills or the sea is choicer than the rest; some mood of passion or insight or intellectual excitement is irresistibly real and attractive to us—for that moment only. Not the fruit of experience, but experience itself, is the end. A counted number of pulses only is given to us of a variegated, dramatic life. How may we see in them all that is to be seen in them by the finest senses? How shall we pass most swiftly from point to point, and be present always at the focus where the greatest number of vital forces unite in their purest energy? To burn always with this hard, gemlike flame, to maintain this ecstasy, is success in life.

—Walter Pater, *Studies in the History of the Renaissance* (1873)

CONTENTS

THE RIDDLE

IT'S FEBRUARY 1999, and I'm motorcycling across the most arid expanse of Burma, now officially Myanmar. The boundless landscape is relieved only by one ribbon of life: the rich river basin of the Aye Yarwaddy that drains the Himalayas and wears a groove through the middle of this starkly beautiful country. My destination is Bagan, an ancient city studded with more than 5,000 temples and stupas over thirty square kilometers. The group I have been traveling with—American bicyclists mostly—are far ahead. Having loaned my bicycle to one of my compatriots whose bike never arrived for the trip, I have been waylaid and detoured pleasantly for hours.

I spot a makeshift taxi ahead, a rickety, Chinese-made truck onto which thirty or so passengers are clinging and clambering. Many of the riders, men and women alike, wear colorful *longyis*—simple pieces of cotton or silk that have been sewn into loops and resemble long skirts—to reflect their tribal affiliations. Most of the women and some of the men have streaked their cheeks, foreheads, and noses with a mudlike paste made from the bark of the thanaka tree, which serves as both cosmetic and sunscreen. Standing on the rear bumper is a young monk, his plum robes pulled over his head to block the sun. He motions toward me, communicating emphatically, if wordlessly. He wants a ride on the motorcycle. I nod in equally silent assent and stop angling to pass the truck, instead trailing it until it stops to lose some and gain some. The monk hops off the truck happily and walks slowly toward me, flashing a warm, penetrating smile. Unleashing my backpack from the seat behind me, I gesture for him to put it on. He dons it and tries to shove a wad of grimy, threadbare bills, *kyat,* into my hand.

"Just get on the back," I say, then realize that he speaks no English. So I wave my palm and shake my head: "No." Gently his hand rests on my shoulder. We take off, quickly overtaking the pickup truck. The monk's robes flutter in the rush of air that gives us both relief from the scorching midday sun. Half an hour down the road, we come upon my cycling friends, lunching at a little roadside inn—a dirt-floored shack, wallpapered with faded posters of Hong Kong beauties and far away beaches. They are clearly amused that I have been adopted by one of Buddha's apprentices. One by one they approach to greet my new companion, meet the insurmountable language barrier, and retreat to their plates of pungent stir-fry.

"You want some lunch?" I ask in a crude sign language that has served me well in my travels.

He shakes his head and slips off to a corner of the table. He might be able to manage one American, but twenty overwhelm him. I offer him a plate of my curry, but he won't touch it, preferring to sip at a sickeningly sweet local soda pop. He waits.

I wolf down my lunch, because I can tell he's ill at ease. He re-dons the pack, and we are back on the motorcycle, tooling down the road. His soft touch on my shoulder lets me know he's still there, but except for the buzz of the two-stroke Japanese engine, we travel without a sound. More endless highway. A scattering of thatched houses on stilts. An occasional open-air market. We slow down for water buffalo pulling a caravan of carts and weave paths around lumbering herds of cattle who wander onto the road, their bells chiming in the dust. At this rate, we won't reach Bagan until after dark.

Half an hour later, the monk signals me, with a tap on the shoulder, to pull over in front of a ramshackle, windowless shed. We enter a crowded room filled with farmers and loiterers, members of a full-fledged profession in Burma. The locals are excited to see an American where none usually tread. The monk sits down at a small bench and offers me lunch. I shake my head. Now it's my turn to wait, sipping green tea, cautiously, not understanding a word that is spoken. He sponges up the last bit of thick, brown sauce with a wad of rice, and we take off again.

Riding for hours, another 100 kilometers or so, we end up at Mount Popa, an ancient Buddhist temple built on a mountain of rock that erupts from an otherwise flat landscape. It's an old, shabby temple, popular with the monkeys. *Nats*, humans who have suffered tragic deaths and have been transformed into animist deities, are worshipped side-by-side with Buddha here and are feted with offerings of fruit, cigarettes, and chewing gum. At night, trance dancers take on the spirits of the Nats in their gyrations.

An older monk in sun-faded robes emerges from the temple's entrance, and the two greet each other with bows. My monk disappears quietly up the hill, without so much as a peep in my direction.

"I'm Mr. Wizdom, the abbot of Mount Popa Monastery," says the older monk. An angular man with day-old stubble on his pate, he wears crooked wire-rimmed glasses that look like they've been mangled and bent back to form many times.

I'm relieved to hear English. I have no idea where the hell I am, my bicycling buddies are long gone, and now I'm almost out of gas.

With the noble hospitality of one who has nothing, Mr. Wizdom motions for me to sit down.

"You know, I picked him up 150 kilometers ago, and I have no idea where I'm taking him?" I say, gesturing toward the one who disappeared. "Is this where he wants to go?"

"Oh, yes, this is where you take him," Mr. Wizdom replies elliptically. We talk briefly, travelers' chitchat, before I ask for and receive directions to Bagan. He hands me a dog-eared card, all unintelligible Burmese except for the odd English phonetic spelling of his name, "Wizdom." Seeing that I'm not rushing to copy down the particulars, he snatches back what must be his one and only calling card. I accept a drink of water and shake Mr. Wizdom's hand. My work is done.

I head back to my motorcycle to find the young monk waiting for me. Confused, I look plaintively toward Mr. Wizdom who is gazing at us from the temple steps.

4

"He wants to go back to where you picked him up," Mr. Wizdom offers with a shrug.

"But you said this is where I take him," I call out.

"Yes, but he wants to go back. Now. Can you take him?" Mr. Wizdom comes forward, a monkey squealing behind him. For his part, the young monk reaches for my backpack, readying himself for another journey.

"But he just got here. I drove him all afternoon. It's nearly sunset. Now he wants to go back? What's the point?"

Bemused, Mr. Wizdom shrugs his shoulders again and turns back toward the temple. "I cannot easily answer that question. But let me give you a riddle to solve." Pausing, he exchanges a smile with the young monk, and turns back to me. I'm wondering how I ended up in a script with a monk named Mr. Wizdom and a magic riddle. "Don't try to answer it now. You must sit with the riddle a while, and the answer will simply come to you."

The truth is I don't much like such games, but the monk doesn't give me a choice in the matter.

"Imagine I have an egg" — Mr. Wizdom cups an imaginary egg in his hand — "and I want to drop this egg three feet without breaking it. How do I do that?"

The monk seems pleased with himself, having mustered enough English to perplex a simple American traveler. My mind flips fast through the forgotten pages of elementary science texts. I am tempted to blurt out answers, for if I solve Mr. Wizdom's riddle, perhaps he will explain what's going on. Instead, I take his instructions to heart and let it go. For now.

With a final nod, Mr. Wizdom retreats, leaving the question with me as a souvenir of Mount Popa. We're back on the motorcycle, me and my wayward monk. This time, the monk leads me to gas. Forget gas stations in rural Burma; instead, dusty bottles lined up at infrequent intervals along the side of the road, each with an old rag stuffed in the mouth like a wick. When you stop to fill up, local merchants mysteriously materialize to take your money.

On we go, yo-yoing silently across the desert. As we approach Bagan, gorgeous brick and stone temples rise up everywhere—some reaching toward the sky, some so tiny you cannot enter without evicting the Buddha in residence. This intricately variegated line of pinnacles and spires is backlit by the fiery red sun dropping into the desert, the Aye Yarwaddy ablaze from the sun's torch.

We keep driving, looking for the old town and my hotel. It has been an exhausting, dusty, hot day on the road, but suddenly I am delighted to be here, at sunset cruising the wonders of Bagan on a motorcycle, a monk on my back. When we first left Mount Popa, I wanted nothing more than to get to my destination, but now I don't have the slightest desire for this trip to end.

The answer comes to me.

Chapter One

THE
PITCH

"WE'RE GOING to put the fun back into funerals."

With that declaration, the meeting began. It was a curious elevator pitch.

"The fun back into funerals?" I asked.

"Absolutely. We're going to make it easy to make choices when someone dies. You know, the casket, the liner, flowers, that kind of thing."

"Fun?"

"Sure. All those decisions. It's not easy. So why not use the Internet?"

"But *fun*? Why fun?"

"Come on. Catchy marketing. You know, a play on words."

"Ah, the *fun* in fun-erals."

"Right. That's it. How many hits do you think you get now if you put the words 'fun' and 'funeral' into Yahoo!? Hundreds? I doubt it. You'll get one, just one. Us."

Giving the pitch is a fellow named Lenny. Something about using the Internet to sell items most people buy at a funeral home when someone dies, items that arouse as many varied and complex feelings as sex toys.

We are seated in the Konditorei, a comfy coffee shop nestled in bucolic Portola Valley. With the Santa Cruz Mountains to the west and Palo Alto and Route 280 to the east, we are but one exit away from Sand Hill Road, the famous home to Silicon Valley venture capital. The Konditorei is where I meet people like Lenny, the pitchmen of the Internet era. Here, or in a couple of restaurants in the same rustic strip mall. This is my office. (Forget Buck's Restaurant in next-door Woodside. That's where venture capitalists prefer to meet supplicants and huddle around deals under a giant painting of Roy Rogers on Trigger rampant. If you sit in the corner of Buck's all morning, starting with the power breakfast crowd, you can quietly observe who is funding whom. It's a voyeur's embarrassment.)

Every morning a stream of humanity stops at the Konditorei for coffee — joggers fueling up, businesspeople in a rush, Stanford students on their way to class, and a handful of deal makers en route from hillside homes to Sand Hill castles. It's also, ironically, a stop for the parade of incoming workers who saw, mow, paint, rake, and hammer away busily at the homes of the Valley shakers. Porsches, Mercedes, and BMW's queue up to enter the freeway, indifferent to the oncoming line of pickup trucks that replace them each morning.

I had arrived a few minutes earlier, and Lenny was waiting for me.

"You're Randy," he began. "I'm Lenny. Frank said you'd be easy to spot."

Shaved head, cowboy boots, jeans, motorcycle jacket—I seldom get mistaken at these blind dates.

With a solid grip, he shook my hand; then, his left hand on my elbow like a politician, he guided me to the table where he'd already set up shop. I could tell by his amped up confidence that he was probably not an engineer. Too outgoing. Too well dressed. So it's not a technology pitch, I said to myself.

I looked at my watch on the arm he didn't have in a power lock. Nine o'clock exactly.

"I hope I didn't keep you waiting," I said. "I had this down for nine."

"Nine is right. Come on," he commanded. "I'll get you some coffee. My treat. You take cream, sugar?"

"Thanks. I don't know what I'll have. Why don't you sit down while I decide."

He started to resist, but I retrieved my arm and walked to the counter. He took one step to follow but then turned and sat down. I let out the breath I'd been holding since he grabbed my arm.

I watched him askance as I waited for my low-fat chai latte, putting his age at twenty-eight. I took stock of his thick, blue-black hair and his pale and drawn face. He looked like he'd been pulling some all-nighters, and by noon he would need another shave. Beneath two smudges of eyebrows, his dark eyes gripped his target like his double-lock handshake—no gazing off and gathering his thoughts. He sat with his body coiled, tense, ready to spring. At me.

9

Lenny's standard-issue corporate uniform—navy blue suit, crisp white shirt, tie a rich mosaic of reds and yellows— pegged him as *not* from the Valley: sales guy, I'd guess. The only one in the Konditorei wearing a suit and tie. Personally I hadn't worn a suit in years. When I was at GO Corporation a few years ago, spending several months negotiating an investment in the company by IBM, my opposite number was one of their seasoned negotiators, Dick Seymour. He was a classic IBM fixer. The equivalent of Foreign Service diplomats, these fixers knew how to manage both the internal IBM organization—all the different inside stakeholders whose interests could often be at odds—and the outside oddballs like us at GO. Seymour was probably in his fifties, fit, highly articulate, utterly professional, and impeccably dressed in a blue suit and crisp white shirt. There I was, in my thirties, in my jeans and T-shirt and florid socks and skateboard shoes, going nose to nose on complicated deal points. Dick treated me like a professional through all our wrangling, not as if I were a creature from a valley of lunatics. GO accepted some tough terms to get IBM's support, but I came away with nothing but admiration for Dick. He had class. He was the consummate deal guy. For all his professional savvy and maturity, though, I couldn't ever imagine a guy like Dick founding a startup.

Now I'm wondering whether Lenny is the corporate type, just younger than Dick and not yet so polished and accomplished.

Connie leaned over the register as she handed me my chai.

"Your friend want another cup of coffee?" she asked.

"I don't know. Sure. You know what he takes?"

"You bet. French roast, black." She whispered, "He's had five cups in the last hour. I'm surprised he can sit still at all. I hope you're wearing your surge protector today." With her sleeves rolled up to handle the morning onslaught, Connie still had time to offer some neighborly advice.

When I rejoined him at his table, Lenny glanced at the coffee I put in front of him and laid a black three-ring notebook in front of me. "Thanks" was obviously not in the script.

"I usually make the presentation on a computer, you know, throw it up on a screen, if I can. That's how Frank saw it. But I checked it out earlier. Too much glare in here. So we'll use the dead tree version."

Here it comes. The pitch. People present ideas for new businesses to me two or three times a week. If I chose to, I could hear a pitch every day—all day, every day. Just as everyone in L.A. has a screenplay, everyone in Silicon Valley has a business plan—most of them nowadays for Internet businesses. I've been around Silicon Valley and involved with young companies since the early '80s—startups, spinouts, spin-ins, what have you. I'm not in the phone book or listed in any professional directory. If you don't know someone I know, you can't find me.

I wonder what Frank had in mind when he set me up with Lenny. I prefer to riff on ideas, brainstorm, prod and provoke, have some constructive give-and-take around a business concept. It didn't feel like there was going to be much of that with Lenny. I gazed out the picture window at the bright California day, the eucalyptus trees rustling in the breeze.

"Before you get started, Lenny, tell me how you know Frank," I said.

"He's, uh, a friend of a friend. We presented to him Monday, and he sounded interested. He wanted us to meet with you right away."

Sounds like the early bird special, a quick chat before Frank and his partners hold their weekly gathering to talk shop and audition new deals. Obviously Lenny didn't know Frank at all. Thanks, Frank. You owe me.

Frank is a headliner in the VC world, whom I've known since I raised money for GO. His firm is "top tier," a term reserved for firms with such a long wake of winners that the mere mention of their names imparts instant credibility and a whiff of inevitability to a startup. We stay in touch. A few days ago he'd called to say he was sending me a prospect. "Intense guy," he confided, "unusual idea but may be 'interesting'. If you like it perhaps we can work together on this one."

"What do you do, Lenny?"

"I sell group life insurance to companies, part of the employee benefit package. National accounts. So I'm out to the West Coast every two or three weeks. I'm the company leader in new sales the last two years. Millions of dollars in value."

Lenny paused a split second and slid some kind of legal document across the table.

"I brought along an NDA. Could you please sign it before I go on." For a second his supreme confidence faltered.

Without a glance, I pushed it back at Lenny.

"I see dozens of companies each month, Lenny. I can't sign a confidentiality agreement. It exposes me to inadvertent liability. My integrity is my stock in trade. If Frank referred you, he can vouch for me. If you're uncomfortable with that, don't tell me anything you think is a trade secret. Frank didn't sign your NDA, did he?"

"Ah, no. I just thought . . . " Lenny said, skidding for a split second. "OK. Let me start."

He flipped open the binder. It was a professional presentation, the kind you see in boardrooms all the time. From his pocket he extracted an extendable pointer. He pulled it out a few inches and tapped at the title page.

"We want to call this business 'Funerals.com,' but some undertaker in Oklahoma already has the URL," he said. "When we get funding we'll buy the rights to the name."

Funerals.com. Oh, brother. What next?

"I understand," I said. Below the title were the date and the words "Presentation to Randy Komisar." He would probably read aloud all the words to me.

"Presentation to Randy Komisar."

"You don't need to read it to me, Lenny," I said. "Just tell me about it."

"Sure, if that's what you'd prefer." He flipped to a page that proclaimed, in a blaze of black type: "The Amazon.com of the Funeral Goods Business."

Now that's a new one.

"This window of opportunity is going to close soon, but if we act now, we can make this the Amazon of the funeral business," Lenny began. "It's going to be big. The world is moving to the Internet—I'll explain that in a minute—and these products will move there too. The Internet's changing the way we live, and it will change the way people die. Someone's going to ride this opportunity all the way to the bank"—or the pearly gates, I said to myself—"and we think we should be the ones."

Next page: "Projected Revenues."

"In the first full year after we're up and running, we expect $10 million in revenue. Fifty million the second year. The third year we really hit our stride—100 million." Lenny paused for effect. "Exciting, right? It's *big*." He waited for my response, then leaned forward and whispered conspiratorially, "Most people don't like to talk about this. Death, dying.

Loved ones passing on. But that's part of the opportunity. You understand that, right? It's a competitive barrier, a hurdle to entry. Most people won't want to do this. Would you?" He looked at me but didn't wait for an honest response. "I wouldn't, if I weren't so damn excited about it."

Until this last line, Lenny's pitch sounded like dozens of others I've heard. Everyone's going to be the Amazon, or the Yahoo!, or the eBay of the you-fill-in-the-blank business. Manifest destiny. Millions—billions even—of dollars overnight. Then sell out, or do an IPO and cash out.

"You know what makes this business so exciting?" he asked.

I waited. The warm spring air wafted through the open doors of the Konditorei.

"People are dying, that's what. It's inevitable. Death and taxes, right? Doesn't matter, rich or poor, what you believe, where you live, how you live, what you think. In the end, everybody has to die sometime, and we're going to be there, ready to provide the goods that people have to buy. They *must* buy! That's the point. You understand? This isn't about eyeballs visiting your site. These aren't eyeballs. These are people who need what Funerals.com has, because everybody dies. And when somebody dies, there has to be one final shopping day to assuage a life of guilt. To buy all these things, expensive things, high-margin things"—he thumped the table and stressed "things" every time he said it—"all these *things*, expensive *things*. And there's no getting around it. These are necessities aimed at the biggest aggregate market in the world—biggest because it includes everyone. *Everyone.*" He paused again for effect. "That's the business, and it's a dream business, because you don't have to convince anybody they need what you have. They know it, brother, they know it. We sell the solution everyone ultimately wants. No demand creation, just redirect it, to *us*."

I looked around the coffee shop sheepishly. Lenny should have asked everyone in the Konditorei to sign nondisclosure agreements. Sure, he might never see these people again, but these are my homies. Connie rolled her eyes. Having overheard so many pitches herself, she knew the drill cold.

Next page: A shaded graph probably sold ready-made in any office superstore in the country. The shameless "Projected Growth" chart inevitably traces the outline of a hockey stick and assumes that a short period of investment will be obliterated by years of exponential increases in whatever — revenues, net income, profits, customers, corpses. Lenny's chart was all about revenues, certainly not profits, because this was, after all, an Internet business.

"Hundred million, three years, easy." Lenny poked his pointer at the highest end of the graph. "Who knows how far it can go. The potential is unlimited, and in three years the exit strategy kicks in. May be an IPO. Depends on the stock market. Probably a buyout."

"Getting to $100 million annual sales in three short years is no small task," I cautioned.

I went on to explain that in the late '80s I'd been one of the founders of a software company, Claris Corporation, that grew to nearly a $90 million annual run rate in three years, and we were profitable to boot. That was when $90 million was $90 million, not like today when $90 million in stock options alone is chump change. I remember all too well how much hard work and good fortune must come together to make that happen.

"Selling software? No offense, but what was that? Hundred dollars a pop? Two hundred? This is thousands of dollars a sale.

Thousands. I'm talking about an order of magnitude difference. No comparison. Besides, the numbers here only include the U.S. You understand that? The U.S. alone. But, people die everywhere, right, not just here? This is truly global. The world market for these goods is at the very least triple, quadruple the U.S. market—tens of billions of dollars, easy."

I pictured some Tibetan ordering the hack-into-small-pieces-and-feed-to-the-vultures economy option. How would Lenny price that?

"Let me tell you something that I absolutely, positively, sincerely believe is the gospel truth." Lenny leaned forward and focused on me with his dark gaze. "You would have to convince me"—he tapped on his chest every time he said "me"—"convince *me* that these numbers are a stretch. A stretch? I don't think so. Listen, somebody's going to do this. No doubt about it. And I say, why not us? *Why* not us?"

Lenny obviously didn't ask questions to get answers, and so I waited through his dramatic pause.

"And I'm not alone in this." He flipped to a page of quotes from analysts and forecasters.

He started to read the first aloud, from Jeff Bezos, founder of Amazon.com, something about "the migration of the $4 trillion global economy onto the Internet."

I held up my hand so I could read in silence. In a world inhabited by people who think the Internet and the universe are converging, no shortage of proselytizers are willing to endorse any kind of cockamamie scheme as the next big thing. But Bezos deserved to be read. I noticed that he made no mention of funerals or caskets.

"Have you been in a funeral home lately?" Lenny said suddenly.

Well, no, I confessed, I hadn't.

"Most people, they'd rather have a root canal. Research reveals that people think funeral homes are creepy places. Not good places for making decisions that can add up to the price of a small car. You're not there because something pleasant is happening in your life. You're there to see someone off, say good-bye. All the queasy questions you never ask yourself in daily life seem to be lurking in the next room, waiting to leap out and grab you by the throat. You know: What happens when you die? Is there life after death? Am I going to be called up next?"

"If you could answer *those* questions on the Internet," I advised, "that would be a great business."

"Oh, there are sites that claim to have the answers, but that's not what we're doing."

Lenny would not be deterred, not with humor, not with questions, not with sidelong glances from strangers at the next table.

"Then there's the guilt: You didn't call enough. You didn't stop in enough. You didn't help enough. Whatever you did, it wasn't enough. Now, by God, your dearly departed dad is going to have the casket of his dreams."

He paused and glared at me, slightly indignant. Was I supposed to be the grieving fool about to spring for the most expensive casket or the conniving funeral director profiteering from human suffering?

"Have you ever heard the pitch?"

"*Your* pitch?"

"No, no. The spiel you get in a funeral home."

"No, I never have."

He brightened. "All right, let me set it up for you. Imagine suddenly somebody's dead."

Again, Lenny had everybody's attention.

"Somebody important to you. You're in shock. Grief has you on your knees. But you're the one who has to make all the final arrangements. So, first, you have to figure out where to go. You've never done this before. It's all new. If you belong to a church or synagogue, you could ask the priest or rabbi. They would probably steer you to one or two homes—and it's not unknown, you know, for the funeral home to give the church a little something in return, by the way—and so you go there. Or you look up the Yellow Pages. Or an acquaintance says she knows somebody had a nice time over to Joe Blow's place. So, tears in your eyes because a light is gone from your life, you head over there. You figure they're all the same anyway, right? First thing, they say, 'We're here to help you.' Help you? I doubt it. They're thinking when you walk through the door, before you walk through the door, about everything they can sell you. Cremation? Sure. How about a $12,000 casket? Let's burn that up too, show some respect. Oh, then there are sealed caskets. I love this. Buy one of those, just a few bucks more, so you can seal the old guy away from all that water and dirt underground. But when you seal it, the anaerobic bacteria can have a feast. Putrefaction sets in . . . ."

A little far, I thought, for an eating establishment. They'll never let me back in.

"Lenny," I interrupted, "it doesn't make sense to go down this road. Just give me the conclusions." I didn't feel like hearing any more of the standard funeral home pitch.

"Wait a minute," someone two tables over called out. "What about those anaerobic bacteria?" Connie shushed him.

"But you've never heard the spiel," Lenny continued. "That's what you said."

"I don't need the experience. Most of your customers won't have had the experience either. If your market is only people who've been suckered in their first funeral, that's not a ready market."

He was undeterred. From his file he pulled out a four-color brochure and spread it in front of me. I suppressed a grin. Even if I did seem to be the sole focus of his sepulchral sell, I had to admire his spirit. He knew what he wanted, and nothing was going to stop him.

I could more than relate to Lenny's single-minded sincerity. Years ago, when I was a young lawyer new to Silicon Valley, I represented a client in an arbitration hearing. Contrary to what you see in the movies or sensational TV trials, many legal proceedings are blandly cordial affairs conducted by lawyers who know each other socially, belong to the same private clubs, and break bread together. Trial histrionics can be as phony as professional wrestling. But I cared very little back then for the lawyer's code of civility. My job was to win for my client, and I was willing to do whatever that took, even if it irritated everybody else in the courtroom. I challenged nearly every one of my opponent's assertions and failed to show respect for my esteemed adversary, a friend of the arbitrator and, unbeknownst to me, a pillar of the local bar association. At the end of the hearing, my boss, the lead partner in the case, turned to me shaking his head. "You're a lawyer's worst nightmare. A guy works all his life to rise above the fray, and you go for the jugular. You don't give a damn, you just want to win." He was bemused and dismayed at the same time. I suppose it's a privilege of youth to be admired and admonished by the wise guys who have gone before.

Lenny pressed on. The brochure showed the latest fashions in caskets: metal caskets in pink and blue with matching satin lining, walnut caskets lined in white satin, and even some Greek sarcophagus-looking numbers. They all had model names, like cars: Peaceful Rest, Solitude, Heavenly Gates.

"Is there one called Hand Basket?" I asked.

"Hand Basket?"

"As in 'Go to hell in a hand basket'?"

He didn't even blink.

"Look at this. Look at this."

He took out two pens and began writing—upside down so I could read what he wrote—dollar numbers next to each casket. It's a trick used by presenters to keep your attention while they write. So far Lenny had shown me his mastery of the Inevitable Growth Curve, and now the magic Upside-Down Writing Trick. Somewhere in his pitch, if I could wait long enough, Lenny would surely reduce the entire world to a four-cell matrix.

Granted, Lenny struggled a little in writing the upside-down numbers, switching back and forth between red and black pens. He wrote two shaky but legible numbers by each casket.

"The red number is the price typically charged by the funeral home," he said finally. Those numbers ranged anywhere from just under $1,000 to several thousand dollars.

"The black number is the cost to the funeral home." Those numbers were all in the hundreds of dollars, some in the low hundreds.

"The margins these guys get are unconscionable. Markups of thirteen, fourteen times cost. They get away with it because nobody feels like shopping around. Everybody thinks funerals have to cost thousands and thousands of dollars. But they don't."

If no one felt like shopping around, I wondered what that meant for his business.

"What margins are you taking?" I asked.

"Good margins, but not rip-offs like many funeral homes. That's the opportunity. We can beat the funeral home prices and still make a tidy profit."

"So this is a price-cutter's business. You're competing on price."

He reached out again and flipped back a few pages.

"Price, convenience, and information. It's the Information Age, and information is what sells on the Internet. We give you the information you need about the product in the quiet of your home. We'll do the price comparison shopping for you in every major city, eventually every city and town. Federal regulations require funeral homes to quote prices over the phone. You don't have to go in person. So we can call them all up and compare what they charge."

He paused. "Sometimes they try to refuse, make it tough, imply you really have to drop by. Those are the sneaky ones I love to get. I used to blast them on the phone, ream 'em. Now I play along, let them refuse. Then I write the FTC and send a copy of the letter to the home. Afterwards, I call up and blast them, only now they got me and the FTC together, kind of a one-two punch, you know?"

Nice business practice. Obviously, something about the funeral industry had gotten under Lenny's skin.

"Pretty compelling, right?" he asked.

One of the regulars at the next table smiled as he rose to leave, carefully folding the business section of *The Merc* and cradling it under his arm. "Very compelling, kid, can I invest?" He winked at me as he walked into the sunshine, offering what was probably the only bite Lenny had gotten on the fundraising trail.

"How do you know people want to make these decisions on the Internet?" I asked.

Lenny beamed. Here comes the Internet pitch, I realized just a second too late. He gathered himself and once again reached over and flipped several pages in the "Presentation to Randy Komisar" binder.

"The Internet changes everything. Why drive to the bookstore to buy a book when you can order it from your couch and receive it FedEx the next day? Why buy airline tickets from your local travel agency when you can take control of your schedule and pricing on-line and accept your e-ticket at the gate? Why buy milk from the local market when you can check off a box on your screen and have it delivered by noon?"

Lenny's rendition of the future made me feel like a prisoner in my own home. "Do you have a graph of Internet profits?" I asked.

Lenny glared at me.

It was a joke. Few Internet companies are willing to discuss profits, let alone produce them. No one knows what a piece of the Internet is really worth, or which economic models will ultimately produce profits, but everyone's betting their patch is rich bottom land, and they're willing to place their bets before anyone has shown they can grow much of anything on it. The market will eventually sort it all out, but the land grab is on.

"You don't get it, do you?" Lenny said. "Let me explain."

With that he launched into yet another rehearsed speech. Obviously he had developed micro pitch modules, and now I was getting the one on the current economics of the Internet, or the lack of them, and why the really smart companies were building brand and staking out territory, at the expense of profits. He said he'd never invest in a company that expected to make a profit in the near future on the Internet. Soon as they make a profit, they've fallen behind. It's growth or profits, etc., etc., etc. I wondered whether there could ever be enough day traders to keep these leaky boats afloat.

While Lenny blasted on, I imagined myself standing outside the Konditorei, looking in through the picture window to see the Pitchman wind up for another inning and wondering how the other guy, me, managed to sit so still as the ball came toward him. My secret was counting my breaths—in, out, in, out—as I planned my escape.

His idea was intriguing in some ways, but it was mostly just another plan for flogging merchandise on the Internet, and esoteric merchandise at that. It wasn't his intensity that irritated me. I expect that in people who found companies. They have to be a little irrational, passionate beyond analysis. If they don't believe in the face of doubt, they'll never make it. But Lenny was operating on automatic pilot set all the way to frantic. I'd have to tell Frank that Lenny and I talked but we never really connected. Frank would have to come to his own conclusions.

A cell phone rang. It wasn't mine—I don't own one. Lenny paused midsentence. For future reference, here was one way to interrupt his relentless pitch. It rang again. He opened his briefcase on the table, snatched out his phone, and snapped it open. "Lenny here," he said, as he strode out the door without a word to me.

Rudeness is as good an excuse as any for an exit. I pulled my jacket off the back of my chair with one last look at Lenny's open briefcase. It revealed a stack of files, an assortment of pens, a family picture stuck on with a paper clip, an economy-size bottle of Pepto-Bismol, and some kind of homemade sandwich—tuna salad?—oozing around the edge of the plastic wrapper. Well, I thought, somebody loves him enough to make a sandwich. Or, maybe he's brown-bagging to save money.

I told Connie I would be back later. She promised to hold my regular table. We both watched Lenny as he sat at one of the tables just outside the open door. Still oblivious to the possibility that someone might overhear, he argued and pleaded into the phone. "Wait! You didn't accept, did you? You said . . . six months. No, one more month . . . we made a commitment."

"Sounds like trouble," Connie said to me.

"Sounds like someone is bailing out," I said.

"No, no, it's too important," Lenny yelped. "Remember what we said after my dad's funeral."

"Aha!" Connie said. "Someone did die. I knew it!"

"No, not a hundred," Lenny argued. "Komisar's only number twenty-six."

"Well," Connie said. "twenty-six? You've moved up. You deserve a better table."

"No, he loves it," Lenny said. "I can see . . . he's in . . . Frank . . . fund it."

"I get it," Connie said. "You're rushing home to get your checkbook, right?"

Now I rolled my eyes.

"Listen . . . one more month. Just a month . . . please. Please. Give me . . ." He was still talking, but, to my surprise, his voice had downshifted, so we couldn't hear him, even as we both strained toward the door. He slumped, wordless, as though the wind had been knocked out of him.

"Is he all right?" Connie whispered to me.

He sat still, his head down, the phone dangling in his hand.

I had to admit this was a different Lenny. For a second, I was a bit worried about him.

Slowly, Lenny sat up and gathered himself. He put the

phone back to his ear and spoke again. The words "two more weeks" were clear enough.

"So, Mr. Last-Chance Twenty-six. You were leaving?" Connie wanted to know. She looked at me hard. "How about another chai?" she asked finally. "On the house."

Perhaps this wasn't the most opportune moment to sneak out. I still had some time before my next meeting, and for all his bravado, this kid could really use a clue.

I took my coat off. "My friend out there," I said, "he'd like a decaf."

Chapter Two

THE RULES OF THE GAME

LENNY, THOUGH SUBDUED for the moment, was likely to spring back to life and resume his story of those putrefying bacteria, probably in the middle of lunch. So, why was I still here?

A couple of reasons, I suppose.

My father's parents were Russian immigrants. My mother's family came off the boat from Germany. Both sets of grandparents left their homelands for a new and unknown world. It was a courageous bet on a vision, simple faith. I see a common gene among immigrants and entrepreneurs who strike out from the pack to pursue their dreams. I admire people who are willing to bet everything on a belief. Some of these risk takers, whether immigrants or entrepreneurs, have a profound impact on what happens in the world. They place bets on the future, often against fantastic odds. I see heroism in that.

The other reason is simpler still. On one or two occasions in my own history I've been helped by people who should have given me the boot for my naïve and disruptive zealotry. I have been sympathetic to the plight of true believers ever since.

I carried Lenny's coffee out to his curbside table. The center's shopkeepers were all arriving for their various businesses—a women's boutique, a video rental-cum-post office, a liquor store noted for its fine wines. Everyone stopped by the Konditorei for their morning java, exchanging pleasantries. No virtual mall could ever replace this small town feel. Technology does have its limitations.

Still preoccupied with his phone call, Lenny was surprised to see me and started to get up. "I'll get the presentation," he said. "We can finish out here."

"Sit down, Lenny. Let's just talk."

"What will you tell Frank?" he asked as he sipped his coffee. Concern and frustration passed over his pallid face.

"I don't really know. If Frank called me right now, I'd have to say I don't completely understand Funerals.com—or you."

Lenny leaned forward to protest, but I cut him off.

"Lenny, I've seen some great ideas—Palm Pilot, WebTV, Intuit. They all struggled in their early days but persevered in the face of many skeptics."

"Struggled? I've got people interested," he countered, obviously eager to reassure himself.

"Any term sheets?"

"Not yet."

"What interest do you have, then?"

"Four or five VCs say it's a great idea. They want me to get back to them when I'm further along. If I can produce a credible lead investor, others will follow."

Ah, it was what I thought. VCs have no percentage in telling you "no" outright. A "no" from a venture capitalist is as rare as the "no" of a Japanese salaryman. Unless you mug the receptionist on the way out or spray graffiti all over their German sedans, VCs seldom turn you down outright.

The other day, a prominent VC described how cutthroat his business had become. One-time friends are bludgeoning each other to win deals. My buddy had gotten cold feet on a deal just as another firm made a move on the founder. "I went crazy to close that financing before it walked out the door," he said. "Wait a minute," I protested. "It was a bad deal." "Sure," he said, "but I couldn't let somebody else steal it."

So, I asked Lenny, why would they tell him "no"? He might improve the idea or his team, or some other investor might get excited and then those on the sidelines would swarm in and create a frenzy. Or, who knows, if not this time, his next idea could be a winner. Might as well keep the door open.

My news was a splash of cold water. Lenny leaned back in his chair. He pursed his lips and shook his head. He had probably suspected as much after all these months, but hadn't been able to admit it to himself or his partner.

"They were still interested," he persisted. "I could tell."

"Listen, why don't we look at Funerals.com the way a VC actually would," I suggested. "A VC asks a set of threshold questions about every business proposal. Let's walk through those, and see where they come out."

I took his silence for assent. I'm sure he would have preferred to finish his pitch, but I didn't give him a choice.

VCs, I explained, want to know three basic things: Is it a big market? Can your product or service win over and defend a large share of that market? Can your team do the job?

VCs like to target markets with big potential, especially tiny markets growing quickly into big markets, like the Internet. If it's a small market, the chance for a portfolio-levitating, reputation-making home run isn't there. A VC's portfolio return is an average of all its investments, so he'd rather have a huge winner and some no-ops than a bunch of minor successes. If you're off-target slightly in a big market, you might still make it, and, if you make it, it can still be big. Off-target in a small market means you're dead.

"So," I asked, "how big is the market for all this funerary gear?"

According to Lenny's research, there are more than two million funerals every year in the U.S. The average funeral and burial costs close to $7,000. That makes a $14 billion market. About a third of that is for the items Funerals.com was slated to sell. That made Lenny's overall market $4 to $5 billion, a sizable target.

"How much of that will be sold on-line, do you suppose?"

"Maybe 25 percent in three years."

"But isn't that a problem, Lenny? Your projected sales of $100 million in three years amount to what share of the Internet slice of that market?"

"Ten percent or so."

"Do you expect a lot of competition?"

"Hell no. Maybe a couple, but we'll be the leader."

"With 10 percent of the market? It doesn't foot."

Perhaps a billion-and-a-quarter-dollar Internet market was too big a guess, but one hundred million in sales suggested he wasn't headed for market leadership. If that was true, it was a problem, because top VCs only want to invest in potential leaders. As most markets grow and eventually consolidate, only the leading one or two players are likely to make money and see their share prices rise. So plans ordinarily promise that the new company will "dominate" its market. If Lenny didn't think this way, VCs would conclude something was wrong with his projections or his ambition. On the other hand, his market share might be much greater than 10 percent, because the total on-line market for funeral gear might be smaller than he projected. Either way, he would have to sort it out.

Funerals.com would face the same issues other Internet retailers face: How much of the market for their goods will shift to the Internet? In the case of Funerals.com, would the business find a way to redirect sales from local funeral homes?

Lenny could only guess. Fundamental to his plan was the assumption that the children of baby boomers would be more willing than their parents to buy these goods electronically. So, following his reasoning, it was important to stake out the territory now and prepare for the growing numbers of baby boomers who will start swelling the funeral market in the next few decades.

Of course, it didn't help Lenny that virtually everyone he'd been talking to, including me, is a baby boomer. We would like to believe we make cool, rational decisions, but not many pitches force the pitchee to contemplate his own mortality.

"So you think it would interest Frank more if we decreased our estimate of the total share of business moving to the Net?" he asked.

"Not necessarily. That could result in too small a target market to be interesting. I assume you estimated your sales bottoms up and projected the market tops down. But either you've underestimated your sales or you've overestimated the potential market. If you don't see yourself as the leader, or you believe the on-line funeral business is pretty small, you won't get much interest."

"But I figured we could show that, even conservatively, we can build a nice, profitable business."

"Fine, but make that the 'worst case' in your plan. Maybe it reduces some risk, but those market share numbers won't inspire investors. Don't even try to do this if you aren't planning to take it all. Then allow for some competitors, but hold the leadership spot. Nothing else is worth investing in."

"Good. That's good." He scribbled notes.

I put my feet up on one of the white plastic garden chairs that serve as café furniture in Portola Valley. When he was done, I asked, "Lenny, why is this a big idea?"

"It's a big market, big dollars."

"Will it change the way the world operates? Will it change people's lives in any meaningful way?"

"Change the world? We're saving some people from the sharks that prey on grief. The current system is awful."

"But basically you're just changing the way the product is sold and bought, substituting yourself for some brick-and-mortar intermediaries."

"What's wrong with that?"

"Nothing, it's probably a good business strategy. How do you see this business in five years, though?"

"$400 million? $500 million!? Who knows?"

"But it's the same thing, right? Same products sold the same way?"

"Yes," he said hesitantly, as though he were missing something. "Is that a problem?" he asked.

"Not necessarily, at least for some VCs," I said. "Let's go

to the second question. What kind of competitive position will you have? What makes your products or services unique and compelling enough to ward off copycats? Can you stake out a significant chunk of your market and defend it? Or can someone reproduce what you're doing overnight?"

Lenny explained that federal regulations aimed specifically at the funeral business created an opportunity for his venture. Funeral homes must accept caskets provided by third parties without fee. The trouble is that the regulations extend that opportunity to everybody, not just Lenny. Like other Internet merchants, he would bank on the limited ability of brick-and-mortar merchants to cut prices. But with these margins, who knows? And what about Internet-based competition? Where were the barriers to entry?

His answers were not satisfactory. He was offering nothing that another competitor couldn't also develop. The key to his business was swift execution. There's nothing inherently wrong with that. But fundamentally, there was a risk that, after Funerals.com gentrified the neighborhood, some brick-and-mortar heavyweight would sweep into town, or some Internet speed freaks would catch Funerals.com from behind. There were no safe havens unless Lenny could achieve Silicon Valley's new mantra, "Build Brand."

"How will people find you when they need you?" I asked. "How will Funerals.com establish a brand and presence? E-commerce is all about distribution, building awareness, being seen, and the Web gatekeepers take a hefty toll before granting you access to their traffic."

His plan was to work with the existing non-virtual infrastructure—social service departments, hospitals, clergy, and hospices—the people who know when someone dies. They would serve as referral points. But would they tell people about Funerals.com? Would that word of mouth suffice in an age of Internet portals?

"Price, convenience, no pressure," he said. "They'll refer people because it's a better way to shop."

"You said a while ago when someone dies, no one wants to shop around," I pointed out.

He made a note, probably a reminder to take that sentence out of his pitch.

"Some won't. Some will," he said.

"Besides, nothing prevents someone else from making the same offer," I challenged. "If that happens, where are you?"

"So far ahead, nobody can catch us," he said.

First-mover status might confer some advantage, but how much wasn't clear. The need to move with ferocious speed is the Internet's legacy. If nothing else, e-commerce forces every business to accelerate to defend its turf or cede precious market share to the fleet-footed mammals of the Web.

"If we beef up that point in the plan, will it make a difference to Frank?"

"You need to address it. It's a threshold question."

He made some more notes. My chai was getting cold. Maybe Connie would be so kind as to warm it up. I turned toward the window and waved to her inside. She ignored me, deliberately not looking my way. No respect.

"That takes us to the third question," I said, turning back to Lenny. "You and your team. Your first-mover status relies on rapid execution. That means the composition of your team is even more crucial than usual, because you won't have time to learn on the job."

"It'll be a good team."

He reached into his case of files and handed me a copy of his business plan. "There's a summary of people in here," he said.

So there was. Unfortunately, besides Lenny, there was only one other founder identified by name. She was a marketing manager for one of the biggest funeral home chains, so she would be the domain expert. He obviously didn't suspect I had overheard his earlier conversation regarding his teammate bailing.

I told Lenny I was troubled by his and his partner's lack of startup experience. It heightens the risk. Startups are unique animals. We take them pretty much for granted out here now, but they are still endeavors that require very different skills from the ones needed in established companies.

Like tourists on safari, senior executives from some of America's largest corporations come to the Valley to study the exotic ways of the natives. Arriving from Chicago or New York or Dallas, they think they need to be more like Silicon Valley startups, but they usually end up scratching their heads. I recently met with some senior managers from a world-class package goods company who had been up and down the Valley. "We thought we could take a crash course in the Valley way and apply the lessons to our business. But this place is extremely foreign to us. We'll have to partner with experienced startup talent and Valley VCs if we really want to try our hand at being entrepreneurial," a senior manager confessed.

Even when large companies try to set up small, intrapreneurial units, they are hard-pressed to find people inside the company who will drive them with the same fervor and penny-pinching zeal that desperation demands of independent startups. The accoutrements of established businesses — the company cafeteria, the clerical support, the illusory job security, the pension plans, and everything else a large organization can provide — are inconsistent with Valley startup mentality.

"I'm not concerned about it," Lenny shot back. "We have a good plan, and we know how to work a plan."

I thumbed through the material. It was a fairly polished presentation: market description, customer need, product strategy, competitive positioning, launch schedule, sales projections, expense forecasts, IRR and other rates of return, investment required, discounted cash flow. All the numbers you'd want. Year one. Year two. Year three. Everything worked out with an inevitable logic. Lenny had outlined in some detail how he planned to run this business.

But how would he react when reality swept over his Power-Point slides?

It was becoming clear that he believed his task was to raise money and then follow his plan. As far as he was concerned, the answers were all there. That's the drill in large companies: "work" the plan. Every week or month or quarter, the head of a new venture will meet with senior management and report progress against plan.

I once sat on the board of a startup that had raised an initial round of funding from a wealthy Hollywood financier. This was the kind of startup the Valley fondly refers to as "Brave New World." (The other kind is more soberly called "Better-Faster-Cheaper.") This particular startup envisioned a business based on a radically new product and service. Naturally the business plan laid out detailed projections, but everything was based on assumptions that could not be tested, short of actually starting the business. Of course, the business at that time was nowhere near the place specified in the plan. Crucial distribution partners were not moving as quickly as expected, and their involvement remained outside our control. The financier, who had made billions in oil and gas, was troubled and became progressively more upset when he learned the company was falling farther behind and away from the plan. He was a savvy investor, but he was not acquainted with technology startups and was increasingly rattled by the risk inherent in this venture.

Finally, after yet another hand-wringing board meeting, at which one of the financier's henchmen screamed, threatened to cut off funding, and jumped management through innumerable hoops, I took the fellow aside. I explained that in a Brave New World startup, where there's no existing market, no incumbent competitors, and no economic model, you're literally inventing the business as you go along. It was absurd, I told him, to hold the team to the original plan. Look at the progress they had made on everything within their control, such as the quality of the organization and the status of the product. It was necessary to be vigilant and flexible in order to learn as the business progressed. These were the right indicia of success at this point, not the plan. The management team was obviously working hard to close a deal with distribution partners and was pursuing alternative strategies. By any measure, except the original plan, this team was doing a great job. The principal use of the plan comes at the beginning, I explained, to show that the founders are intelligent, capable of structuring the business concept and expressing a vision of the future. Later the plan can help track problems that may reflect on the startup strategy itself. The financier's henchman calmed down, but his boss never really got the point; he dropped out before the company went on to be sold for more than half a billion dollars.

"Lenny," I said, "I doubt your plan will take you all the way. There are too many unknowns. You'll need people capable of navigating without street signs. The composition and experience of the team are something VCs will look at hard."

VCs invest first and foremost, I explained, in people. The team would have to be intelligent and tireless. They would need to be skilled in their functional areas, though not necessarily highly experienced. Moreover, they would need to be flexible and capable of learning quickly. Heaps of information about the market and the competition would be streaming in after they launched. They would have to course-correct, on the fly. Refine the strategy, maybe even radically. This team would have to be comfortable with uncertainty and change. That's why VCs look for people with some startup experience, people who have proven they can thrive in chaos. It significantly reduces the risk of failure.

"If we can get a VC to put in the money," Lenny said, "and then work with us to fill in the gaps in our experience, we should be all right."

If Lenny was relying on the VC to provide the startup experience his team lacked, he was confused about venture capitalists and their role. He wasn't alone.

Venture capital firms have a great business—the investment business. They bring in money from limited partners, and it's their job to give back to those limited partners a return that reflects the risk taken with that money and exceeds what they are likely to get from other investments. For that effort, the VC gets a fee and a carry, a percent of the deals gratis.

In the early days, VCs often rolled up their own sleeves to make their investments successful. Many had come from operating roles and could actively contribute to the businesses they funded. The total money they had to invest was trivial by today's standards, which meant they could make only a handful of investments annually, a manageable number that allowed them to bring their experience with their money to each venture.

Today's funds are huge in comparison, sometimes approaching a billion dollars. Because of this size, VCs now need to invest larger amounts of money in more companies to produce the returns that attract investors. It's not uncommon for a VC partner to sit on a dozen or more boards. To that they have to add the hefty demands of running their own businesses. Consequently most VCs (even if they insist otherwise) simply don't have the time to give close management attention to the companies they've funded. In addition, in contrast to the original VCs, who often gathered years of operating experience prior to becoming venture capitalists, many partners in today's firms have no executive management experience. They could be working on Wall Street as easily as on Sand Hill Road.

With frenetic energy and a natural penchant for risk taking, these armies of prospectors are smart, hardworking, and aggressive. They do bring connections and contacts to the aid of the companies they fund, in addition to money. Often stereotyped as "vulture" capitalists who drive expensive cars, drink pricey wines, collect extravagant toys, and wish they had the time to indulge in their expensive hobbies, they are reminiscent of Wall Street masters of the universe, or L.A. players—except for one thing: their bets build the future in remarkably tangible ways. While their N.Y. and L.A. counterparts feast on marbled steaks from the corner butcher, VCs birth, fatten, and butcher their own steers before the barbecue. Take them out of the picture, and the Valley and its financial boom collapse. A few of the venture capital firms are beginning to recognize the limitations of the current "stretched thin" situation, and there are, of course, some notable exceptions to the present trend. Regardless of the amount of attention they can spend on any single company, they are still some of the heroes of the new economy.

Nevertheless, for the past few years there has been no shortage of capital and new ideas in the Valley. Management talent has been the limiting factor. Startups require an odd mix of skills and personalities. Many top tier VCs use their credibility to attract big-name talent from corporate America, with the promise of huge payoffs in the Valley. This can ensure that a new venture sails smoothly out the gate. But when a small startup runs into trouble early—and many, if not most, do—carpetbaggers more accustomed to managing a multibillion-dollar business may find they just don't have the skills to make a startup work. Anyone can sail with the wind to his back. Startups usually sail into a stiff wind, leaking like a sieve, in high seas, without food or water. If Lenny got the money he wanted for Funerals.com, he would face that problem right away.

"How committed is the other founder?" I asked.

For the first time, Lenny deflected his gaze as he spoke. "She'll join soon as we can raise enough money."

Was he lying to me or deceiving himself?

"Remind me how much you're looking for," I asked.

"Five million dollars to build the basic service and distribution network, develop relationships with manufacturers, and flesh it all out. We could roll out in six months."

Not an unreasonable amount, and consistent with the VC's need to put a lot of money into each deal. "Five million dollars at what valuation?"

"Twenty-five million."

"Good luck." I shook my head. Lenny was deluding himself. He was looking for a large valuation so he could raise his financing by selling the smallest percentage of the company possible, thus maximizing his ownership. The Valley calls that minimizing "dilution."

"Fifty million in sales the second year will make that a bargain. And I can quote comps."

"Lenny, you have an idea, a cofounder, and a business plan. Nothing earthshaking or inherently valuable like an exclusive market or a key patent. No track record. You need to reset your expectations."

I had to explain. Valuation is all about risk and reward. Sure, $50 million is a sizable business, but what are the chances for failure or delay? And how much money would he ultimately need to be successful? Future dilution would have to be figured in the mix. The lead VC is more likely to want around 40 percent of the deal for his money at this stage.

If Lenny were to raise $5 million, 40 percent would mean that the post-money valuation, the value of the company plus the new money, would be more like $12.5 million. Subtract the investment, and you have a $7.5 million pre-money valuation, the implied value of the business. Nowhere near the $25 million Lenny was suggesting.

Everybody here brags about valuation, but Silicon Valley really operates on momentum. Many times I caution a company not to take the largest valuation they can in a financing, because it sets the wrong expectations and probably attracts the wrong investors. Peg the round at the highest reasonable price necessary to raise the desired amount from the *right* investors. The right investors bring credibility, experience, and networks. They support you with enthusiasm in later rounds. They raise your valuation merely by their presence in the deal.

The right amount to raise is a range with a minimum, but seldom a relevant maximum. In a fiery market like ours, raise enough for a year's burn rate, or net loss, assuming the worst.

41

Then add on enough for another six months, and take anything reasonably offered above that. I have never seen a company fail for having too much money. Dilution is nominal, but running out of money is terminal. Set reasonable expectations among your investors, don't gouge them, and then out-perform expectations. Future rounds will be much easier if you are seen as having positive momentum.

If you are fixated on dilution, you can take less cash and focus maniacally on meeting critical milestones in order to raise your valuation before soliciting more investment and experiencing further dilution. But beware that you risk under-performing or, even worse, falling prey to changes in market attitudes or conditions that may make future rounds more expensive or even impossible to raise. If you hit a snag, your precious momentum goes out the window. The current euphoric markets make it advisable to take all the money you can while the bloom is on the rose.

Lenny took more notes. Two friends of mine noisily entered the Konditorei, deep in argument. Tom insisted that eBay was a buy at $150 per share. Steve was incredulous, as always, muttering about the tulip craze in seventeenth-century Amsterdam. Their debate revived itself daily without ever producing an apparent winner. Tom had made millions investing in Internet startups in the past few years. Steve had probably scraped by on a balanced diet of blue chips and mutual funds, but he insisted he'd get the last laugh. They grabbed their takeout orders and waved as they left, aware that the door to my office was, for the time being, closed.

"Lenny," I said, "you mentioned your exit strategy, selling out or doing an IPO in three years or so."

"More likely a sale." His explanation held little surprise, since the way to create a retailing business on the Web has become fairly straightforward. Raise money. Build a site, where you offer attractive, fun, and informative content, as well as a wide choice of steeply discounted products. Focus entirely on growing sales and your customer list at a phenomenal rate. Expand your product lines. Grow even faster. Go public. Profits and margins be damned. According to Lenny's logic, an established e-tailer suffering from negative margins might eventually be interested in acquiring niche lines of high-ticket, higher-margin products like his funeral gear. Most likely, he said, he would sell Funerals.com in two or three years to one of the larger Web retailers.

Personally I could not fathom Amazon selling caskets, but that wasn't important now. There was a bigger issue here.

"That's an exit strategy for your investors. Is it one for you too?"

"For me too?" He seemed confused by the question. After all, wasn't he an investor?

"Is that your personal exit strategy? Are you planning to get out?"

"Yes. Of course."

"If you raise money and do this," I asked, "but it doesn't work quite like you planned, and you don't get the gold, or silver, or even brass ring, will you think it was a waste of your time?"

"It would be a disappointment," he said. He didn't say he would consider it a total failure, but that was the message in his voice and on his face when he spoke.

I thought about that for a second. Lenny was clearly mystified by my questions. "All right," I said. "I think I have a better sense now of what you have in mind. I'll talk to Frank."

"What will you tell him? Are you onboard?"

Am I onboard? That was the question. The market is huge

and rather unusual. Lenny's plan demonstrated that he knew his beans about the business of dying. Iffy, but who knows? Funerals.com might be a big success.

"I'll tell Frank it's probably worth going to the next step and doing some due diligence," I said. "He'll raise many of the same questions I did about your people and your ability to build some sustainable advantage. You'll have to see where that leads."

"That's great!" Lenny leapt up from the table, hopefully. "So you basically like it?"

"I think Frank should go the next step."

"Then you'll work with us?"

With a "yes" and a handshake, I could show Lenny a faint ray of light, after weeks and months of gloom.

"I don't think so, Lenny."

His jaw dropped a fraction, and disappointment washed over his face.

Chapter Three

THE VIRTUAL CEO

SOME PEOPLE CALL ME AN ANGEL. In the world of startups, angels invest in seed or early-stage deals, and with their money they lend a bit of advice. They pay for the privilege of helping the company. But I'm no angel.

This was a point of confusion for Lenny. He'd assumed I was just some kind of newfangled Silicon Valley investor.

"But your VC analysis suggests that Funerals.com is worth a closer look," he protested when I declined his invitation. "That's what you're telling Frank. Why wouldn't you do the same?"

"I don't necessarily look at things the way a VC does," I

said, seeing that my comments were tripping him up. I've worked in Silicon Valley since the early '80s. I understand how it functions and thinks, but I don't necessarily see things the same way.

"If you're not interested in helping us, Frank won't be," Lenny said unhappily.

"Did he say that?" I asked. It sometimes happened. A VC, concerned about the lack of experience among a group of founders, might ask them to involve a little gray hair (or, in my case, a shaved head) with some startup management credentials.

"Not in so many words, but I thought if you invested . . . "

Sometimes I do put money into companies, but generally not in the startups I work with. If I invest, I am prone to think like an investor, favoring my return over what's best for the team and often its long-term business.

I explained to Lenny what I do: I incubate startups. To that end, I provide the scarcest commodity of all, leadership and experience. I help the people build their ideas into successful businesses. Neither an angel nor a consultant, I support entrepreneurs as a kind of junior partner, a full member of the team, an owner and a decision maker, not a hired hand. I invest my time, and, in return, I receive an equity stake in the business. With that stake, I think like a team member, and sink or swim with the founders.

Some people call me a virtual CEO. When Steve Perlman founded WebTV a few years back, I agreed to help him get started, first as an advisor, and then as a member of his board. Gradually I became more active in the business, but I declined to assume a traditional role as an executive in the company. One day in 1996 Steve presented me with business cards that read "Randy Komisar, Virtual CEO, WebTV."

The title stuck. I started working with a handful of companies at a time. I generally devote myself to each for a year, perhaps two. In that period we should be able to raise money, develop the product or service, identify the market, create a business model, prove out its basic tenets, and hire an operating team. With that team in place, I retreat to an advisory capacity and give more hands-on attention to the next startup.

My specific work in each of the companies depends on the backgrounds of the founders and the particulars of the business. My work is improvisational. Though involved in all the planning and major decision making, I don't play any day-to-day operating role. On the org chart I'm a bubble around the management team. Startups require frenetic execution and relentless perseverance. My role is to keep my head out of the cyclone and provide insight, direction, and stability. I try to bring to each company the experience I've gained—raising money, setting strategy, building and leading teams, establishing strategic relationships, developing products and services and bringing them to market, doing deals. And I make available to the startup all my contacts in the industry.

Good entrepreneurs are passionate visionaries, usually with one or more exceptional talents, but rarely have they actually built a company from scratch. I fill in the gaps in their experience. The actual CEO is ultimately responsible for all the company decisions. As a Virtual CEO, I simply provide the team with guidance and leadership when necessary. I can be very outspoken, if I fear that we don't have room for a misstep. But the CEO is in charge; I'm there to make him or her successful.

When I advise a startup, the business for me *is* the founders. It's an expression of their collective vision. As a director of a publicly held company, I accept a fiduciary duty to the investors, but in a privately held startup I don't favor the investors over the founders. This is probably the crucial way my thinking differs from a VC's.

"Lenny, let's be clear on a few points here," I said. "I need to understand why you're starting Funerals.com in the first place."

"To prove I can succeed in this startup game," he said. "And to get rich, why else?"

"OK," I said, "but what will you do if you make the money? You have to do something, you're too young to clip coupons."

He shrugged. "There are other things I want to do."

Ah—the crux of the matter.

"There's nothing wrong," I said, "with cashing out and making a lot of money—unless those 'other things' you intend to get to are what you'd rather be doing all along."

I pointed at his plan. "My experience tells me if you do this for the money, you'll just end up howling at the moon. The money's never there until it's there. There must be something more, a purpose that will sustain you when things look bleakest. Something worthy of the immense time and energy you will spend on this, even if it fails."

He began rearranging his files, giving himself busywork, time to think.

"What am I missing?" finally erupted out of him. "Isn't that how it works out here?"

"Lenny, that approach simply isn't interesting to *me*. I don't have time to invest in merely building bank accounts. I realize as much as the next guy that the average startup will be acquired. By any calculation, there's no call for the number of independent companies that we're creating in the Valley. Many are simply products or services masquerading as companies. I can accept that as the dictate of the market, but I can't muster the energy for a company whose founders never hope to accomplish anything more than making some bucks. By setting your expectations low, you almost guarantee mediocrity."

The Konditorei had filled with the din of young children. One or two of the kids ran around berserk, their Nordic nannies chasing after them. I spotted an old friend, Sarah, from my time at Apple in the mid-1980s, and got up to give her a hug. She lives nearby with two small children now, married to one of the ex–vice presidents of engineering during the Sculley regime. She loves to ride horses, but the kids seem to occupy all of her time. I only run into her here, at the Konditorei. Whenever I see her quickly growing children I marvel at how much time has passed. Better watch out. I had never planned to grow old in this Valley.

I introduced Sarah to Lenny and then sat back down as she walked to her car, threatening to really get together one of these days.

"You know," Lenny said, "I have to tell you, I don't get this at all. I thought you'd just say you didn't like the products. Too creepy. Or you didn't like my tie. But this is Silicon Valley. Where you go to get rich."

Yeah, yeah. The entrepreneur's casino. Everyone knows the score. Get the venture money and return it at rates that make a loan shark misty-eyed.

"I'm not talking about Silicon Valley," I reminded Lenny. "You asked if I was interested, remember? This is how I look at a business."

Lenny raised an eyebrow. He must have felt like he'd stumbled into some renegade lodge of Freemasons. He thought he'd learned the secret handshakes, the passwords, the arcane rituals. But what he'd learned obviously wasn't working on me.

"Are you saying I shouldn't be doing this?" he asked accusingly. "You telling me to give up? Is that what you think?"

"Not at all. I never tell anyone to quit," I said. "I may not want to be involved, or I may think your idea is likely to break your heart and your bank account, but I never say quit."

"Then I'd like to know your opinion. If we get the money, even if you don't join us, what do you think of our chances?"

"Lenny, your plan calls for raising as much money as possible and then launching your business as soon as possible. You predict an opening in the on-line market for these funerary goods, and you need to fill that hole quickly and completely."

"Right," he said. "It's that Internet land rush. If we're going to dominate the market, like you say, we'll have to sprint, even if we start today."

Lenny's eagerness to charge ahead was laudable. It certainly matched the way the Valley now works. Over the last several years, with more money, more deals, and less attention paid to any single company, a new investment model has taken hold. Fill each startup with rocket fuel as fast as possible and blast it into space. The ones that fly, fly, and if the rest of them blow up, c'est la vie.

"It's not quite that simple," I quipped.

"What are you saying?" Lenny wanted to know. "We shouldn't move quickly?"

"Lenny, you're selling known products to an existing market. Your competitors—at least your brick-and-mortar competitors—are identifiable. That all says you're probably a Better-Faster-Cheaper startup, and your goal is to unseat the brick-and-mortar incumbents. Your biggest bet is that people will buy these things on-line. A big bet indeed, but there is no brain surgery in it. So the rocket ship model is probably the right one for Funerals.com. You should get on and go as far and as fast as possible."

"Then what's the problem?"

I explained that there are two issues. The first faces all Web rocket ships. We're awfully early in this market to be declaring the first-movers the victors. Our perspective is too short, and it colors the lessons we think we're learning. 3DO was a first mover in the so-called next-generation video game business, yet it was completely overrun by later entrants Sony and Nintendo. And that's just one example I happen to know firsthand. It's not clear that being the first-mover will provide the rash of Internet startups a sustainable competitive advantage. Ultimately being right, or better positioned, may be more important than being first. "Your second hurdle," I told Lenny, "is that, in spite of all that's known about your products and market, you still face some big unanswered questions."

As happens with most startups, Lenny's plan raised questions that couldn't be answered until he actually launched Funerals.com. How many people will buy funeral goods on the Web? For goods evoking so many layers of complex emotion, can you do without human contact? What's the market segment that will respond on the Net, and what are the specific products and services those people want? What's the best way to attract customers? How will you work with local funeral homes to ensure a satisfactory experience for customers?

"None of those answers is obvious, Lenny," I said, "but each answer is crucial to your success. Your rocket may fly in the wrong direction and blow up, or run out of fuel."

Lenny was skeptical. He had no trouble naming a half dozen rockets that flew just fine.

In fact, the Rocket Ship Model of startup investment has recently produced many of the most prominent Valley successes. But for every one of them, there are many potentially viable companies that might have eventually prospered if they had been incubated longer.

When too much money is pumped too fast into a startup, there's no room for mistakes. The initial product and the initial fix on the market have to be right. There's no way these companies can stop and reconsider what they're doing without a great deal of pain. They lose momentum, and that sense of momentum—in terms of market acceptance, financing opportunities, partnership interest, and the ability to attract talent—is crucial in the Valley. The dreaded "restart"—writing down a company's value and raising new money around a fresh direction for the business—means all the previous work was for naught. Everyone loses, especially the founders. More often the walking wounded are simply sold off for the value of their assets, or scuttled entirely.

Some startups, Brave New World startups especially, need to proceed more gingerly, because there are no precedents to guide them. They need to feel their way for a while, operate by trial and error. In those cases, my approach is different, because my goal is to optimize the company, not maximize a portfolio. Take one of the startups I'm working with right now. It's offering a new kind of marketing and promotion service on the Internet, but how and when the market is going to develop—who knows? A typical VC might have pounded money into this business and forced it to ramp up before it had enough experience with customers and the service to aim properly. My advice? Stay small and remain flexible for the time being, so we can keep close to the market, learn from prospective customers, and afford to take some missteps. You have to be able to survive mistakes in order to learn, and you have to learn in order to create sustainable success. Once the market is understood and the product is fully developed, then move fast and hard. If, on the other hand, we discover with this approach that there's no market after all, we won't have wasted truckloads of money.

"Don't get me wrong, Lenny," I said. "I'm all for moving fast. There are times when the rocket ship is the right way to go. It may be the right way to go for Funerals.com. I'm only saying it's not necessarily the case. That's an important question for you to confront."

I looked at my watch and saw it was time to move on. I stood up.

The Konditorei was in its midmorning lull. Only a few real estate agents were coming in to perk up with some caffeine before confronting their first desperate clients of the day. Selling million-dollar teardowns and multimillion-dollar fixer-uppers could take it out of you. Luckily demand far outstrips supply in this market. After the first dozen curb calls, you could usually count on hungry home buyers to knuckle under, feeling thankful for the privilege to bid on condemnable estates. I recognized one of the agents and nodded hello.

"Hey, Komisar," he said, "I have just the thing for you, a very private, charming Asian-inspired place on the ridge. Terrific view, not even listed yet. I could get you in for a peek."

"Sam, I have enough to worry about without taking on a new house. I haven't paid for the one I'm in yet. Look around for another 'motivated' buyer. You may even have to get out of your chair to sell this one."

Lenny reached over for the business plan that was still on the table. His hand on the document, he tried one more time. "Why don't you take a copy of the plan. If you have the time, I'd appreciate talking to you about it again."

I accepted the package, knowing there was almost no chance I would ever get back to it. I hear one hundred plus pitches a year, and I can only commit to a handful.

"I'm not discouraged," he said as he reassembled his materials. "I've had problems before, and I've solved them."

"I'm glad to hear that," I said. I meant it. Lenny had that entrepreneurial spirit. He had the determination and sheer willpower to turn mountainous obstacles into speed bumps.

He reopened his file case and withdrew a thick folder. I read the label: "Business Plans." It was full of documents, a couple of inches thick. He hefted it, testing its weight.

"I've done six, no, seven versions of the plan," he said. "Every time I make a presentation and someone asks a question not covered in the plan, I address it. I'll revise the plan on the plane tonight, improve it."

A gust of wind whipped the pages open.

"Out of curiosity, Lenny," I asked, when he had the pages under control, "how'd you pick this idea, funeral goods?"

"It's a huge brick-and-mortar market with a lot of problems. I figured the Internet might offer a chance to take advantage of those problems. Besides, it's a horse race, and all the other horses are slow." Or dead, I mused. I resisted jokes about the glue factory.

His answer sounded slightly glib.

"You mean you looked around for a good Internet business to start, and *this* was it?"

He hesitated while he put away the folder. "Let's say I had some, uh, experience with a funeral home."

He clasped his hands in front of him on the table and looked at them.

"So it's revenge too," I said.

He considered that for a moment. "I like 'justice' better."

He slid back in his chair and stood up, looking me directly in the eye.

"Pardon a personal question," he said, "but from what Frank told me, I guess you've done all right. So—if I may— before I leave, let me turn this around. If it's not the money, why do *you* do this? Why are you still breaking your back around here?"

"That's not an easy answer," I said, and I tried to explain.

It comes down to my realization over the years that business isn't primarily a financial institution. It's a creative institution. Like painting and sculpting, business can be a venue for personal expression and artistry, at its heart more like a canvas than a spreadsheet. Why? Because business is about change. Nothing stands still. Markets change, products evolve, competitors move into the neighborhood, employees come and go. There's always the "son of Lenny" to threaten all you hold dear.

Business is one of the last remaining social institutions to help us manage and cope with change. The Church is in decline in the developed world, ceding leadership to a materialism of unprecedented proportions. City Hall is subservient to the economic interest of its constituencies. That leaves business. Business, however, has a tendency to become tainted with the greed and aggressiveness that at its best it channels into productivity. Left to its single-minded pseudo-Darwinian devices, it may never deliver the social benefits that the other fading institutions once promised. But, rather than give up on business, I look to it as a way, indirectly, of improving things for many, not just a lucky few. I accept its limitations and look for opportunities to use it positively. In the U.S., the rules of business are like the laws of physics, neither inherently good nor evil, to be applied as you may. You decide whether your business is constructive or destructive. I help people understand this and express themselves in what they do, trying to make a difference through business.

It probably wasn't the answer he expected. He chuckled.

"Creative? Personal expression? Making a difference?" he mused. "Must be nice, but that's not my experience. I can't remember how many ideas I've brought into my company that have gone nowhere. We fight for the bottom line. 'Beat the numbers. Beat the numbers.' I've given up. So I play the game, do my job."

No wonder he was hawking a startup.

"I didn't say every business situation is creative or constructive," I responded. "I only said business at its heart has the potential for creative expression and positive change."

He rubbed his hands as if they were cold.

"I really wish that were true," he said. "But I've never seen it."

"It took me years to understand it," I said. "It's not obvious."

I pulled on my leather jacket. We shook hands. He stood by my bike as I put on my helmet and revved the engine.

He seemed at a loss for what to say. Another frustrating day. No money. His cofounder bailing out.

"I'd like to stay in touch on this, if that's OK?" he asked.

"Send me an e-mail. That's the best way."

I slowly pulled away from the curb. Lenny and I would probably never see each other again. Nonetheless, I wished the best for him. Another short-timer struggling to do something he hoped would, if it succeeded, clear the way for what he really wanted to do, whatever that was. In my rearview mirror I glimpsed him standing alone at the curb, briefcase in one hand, file case in the other.

Chapter Four

THE DEFERRED LIFE PLAN

I ARRIVED BACK HOME LATE that evening after dinner with some old friends at the Iberia, another of my local spots. It was a bit of a "My Dinner with André" gathering. We postulated, between the paella and a few bottles of Spanish wine, on just how high the market could go and wondered whether there would be a bottom if things deteriorated. By my second glass, I was holding forth on the metaphysics of business, the human and social dimensions of commerce. My companions—all variously involved in the Valley as founders, funders, or functionaries—had heard this bit so many times, they just nodded in faint agreement and tried to steer the conversation back to the practicalities of buying low and selling high.

My afternoon had divided neatly into two parts: First back at the Konditorei for another pitch from a group of upstarts proposing to use the Net to improve customer service, retention, and recovery. Then a board meeting at which, depending on how you wanted to look at it, we wrestled with an impending cash crunch or we readied the company for a public offering. What looks like a cloud to one person is a chance to sell umbrellas to the next.

My wife, already off to bed, had left a light on. Debra is a high-powered senior executive at Hewlett-Packard, now one of the Valley's most venerable companies, decades beyond its scrappy start. Tika and Tali, our more-or-less Rhodesian Ridgebacks, shoved their muzzles through the door as I opened it, their tails drumming the wall in unison.

I ditched my boots, poured myself a Calvados, and headed to my office for the final task of the day: clearing phone messages and e-mails. Through the window, the distant lights of San Francisco twinkled like the Milky Way.

My first message was from Frank.

TO: <u>randy@virtual.net</u>
FROM: <u>frank@vcfirm.com</u>
SUBJECT: Dead or Alive?

Randy, any chance yet to talk to the Funerals.com guy? Unusual idea. Lemme know what you think.

Frank

A sandy-haired, softening, former fraternity boy out of UCLA, Frank is a genuinely nice guy. But his easy affability hides a fierce competitive streak. On the brink of forty, he's been in the business for more than a decade. He knows as well as anyone that it is important first to evaluate every aspect of a new idea with analytical precision but that, in the end, the decision to fund or move on is a matter of instinct. Frank can apply all the right metrics, but it is his nose that gives him his edge. He has a deep respect for entrepreneurs, coupled with a no-nonsense attitude toward performance. He would pull his support in an instant if he felt a founder wasn't cutting it.

Until Frank's note, though, my morning with Lenny had become a distant memory. Funeral goods. Bacteria. Make it big, then cash out.

I hit "Reply" and tapped out an answer:

TO: frank@vcfirm.com
FROM: randy@virtual.net
SUBJECT: Re: Dead or Alive?

We missed you at dinner tonight. All the usual suspects and the usual conversation--denigrating your portfolio and discounting your returns as the blessings of an innocent. I tried to defend you, but it was futile.

As for Funerals.com, the funeral goods market appears to be huge, so it merits some serious consideration. Lenny himself seemed bright, energetic, and driven, and also naïve and inexperienced. He doesn't have a team. His plan is fairly polished but incomplete, and his strategy limited--lots of fundamental

```
issues still to be resolved. All in all,
I didn't find anything here of particu-
lar interest to me, but you might do
some more due diligence because of the
market potential.

best

r
```
_____

I looked the note over. I wanted to be honest and fair.
Lenny was hard to read. His drive and desire were plain to
see, and he had the makings of a good promoter, but something was missing.

Yawning, I hit "Send" and then deleted Frank's e-mail.
Case closed.

I worked through the remaining messages one by one—
FYIs from some of the companies I work with, a few queries
from friends of friends suggesting we meet to discuss new
ideas, and one from my sister the accupuncturist in Boston
letting me in on a new herbal remedy. Then an e-mail from
Lenny. I noted the time; he'd sent it well after midnight in
Boston.

```
TO: randy@virtual.net
FROM: lenny@alchemy.net
SUBJECT: Thank You

Randy,

Many thanks for meeting with me this
morning. I learned a lot from your
reactions, and I revised the
Funerals.com plan on the flight home.
It's stronger now, with your help.
```

Thanks.

I hope you'll have a chance to look at the revised business plan I've attached. I incorporated the changes you suggested. It's a huge market, and someone is going to make a killing in it.

Let me know any thoughts about the new plan. I hope you'll reconsider working with us.

Thanks again.

Lenny

I replied:

TO: lenny@alchemy.net
FROM: randy@virtual.net
SUBJECT: Re: Thank You

I appreciated hearing about Funerals.com this morning. I've passed on my thoughts to Frank, as I said I would. You're right. Someone will figure out the on-line market for funeral goods.

Thanks for your interest in my working with you, but as I said at the Konditorei, I can't get excited about a business whose biggest idea is making money. Nothing wrong with that, but it's not where I want to invest my time. That's a personal choice, not a judgment.

```
Good luck.

best

r
```

I finished off the remaining three e-mails and thought, finally, I was done for the day. Then a ping—a reply from Lenny. I looked at my watch. It was almost 3:00 A.M. in Boston. The guy must not sleep.

```
TO: randy@virtual.net
FROM: lenny@alchemy.net
SUBJECT:Re:Re:Thank You

Randy,

Thanks for your quick reply. I'm disap-
pointed but understand, I think.

If you don't like Funerals.com, that's
fair, but I have to confess I left our
meeting feeling I had somehow misled
you. Your reply makes me sure of it.

All you know about me is Funerals.com,
and I wouldn't want you to believe
that's all I'm about. While I think of
myself as a hard-nosed businessman, and
Funerals.com is meant to be a business,
I'd be upset if I left you with the
impression that I'm merely a greedy
opportunist. You saw only my business
side. There's more to me than that, and
I'll get to it after Funerals.com is a
great success.
```

```
I hope you'll check out my site--URL
below. It should give you a little more
insight into me.

I still look forward to a chance to
meet again. If you have any further
thoughts, I'm all ears.
Lenny
```

I had indeed pegged Lenny as a greedy opportunist, but I hadn't expected, in the heat of all his bluster, that he was astute enough to register my impatience. Curiosity overpowered sleepiness. What the heck—I checked out his URL.

Adorned with digitized Polaroids of parents and siblings, Lenny's Web site took me back to the early days and all the commotion over the vast and messy democratizing eloquence of the Net. Every voice and community would have a place in cyberspace. The Web would foster paeans to the special talents of the family hamster, hipper-than-thou e-zines run by semiotics students, and gritty neighborhood joints for all manner of hobbyist. Shoot the middleman, free the masses.

All these highly charged, highly personal sites left you feeling a little strange at first, as though you were picking through the effects of another's life, peeking at someone's diary. I felt the same way looking at Lenny's site, even though he had invited me.

Lenny had quite a family—three brothers and a sister— each lovingly accounted for with pictures commemorating major life events: grammar school with its annual, grainy head shots; Scouts; the goofy haircuts of the seventies; high school proms; weddings; cheery toddlers with arms outstretched toward the camera. Nothing special here—just another family with its intimate history frozen in an uncomfortably public way.

About to call it a night, I noticed another picture. The characteristic black hair gave away the man's identity—Lenny's father, Jack Dolan.

Clicking on the photo opened a memorial site for Lenny's father, who had died almost eight months earlier. I recalled what Lenny had told me in the Konditorei. There were more family photos—Jack with each of his children and his wife—some pages of text, and, under the heading "At Play," a group of pictures showing Jack Dolan working in a garden that was a riot of color. One photo showed him standing by a stretch of forsythia. Another showed him with spade and hoe, crouched over a flower bed, planting seeds in this suburban Eden. He was always smiling, hands working the earth in front of a small, one-family Cape Cod. Every corner and window was festooned with flowers like some intricately designed English garden. This house must have been the neighborhood attraction. Under the heading—"Taking Care of Business"—I came across a few more photos: Jack Dolan posed soberly behind a tidy desk or engaged in serious-looking work, his dark jacket framing a white shirt and a quiet tie. He was described variously as a "dedicated public servant" and a "faithful friend of the Commonwealth"—by the Governor, no less—and commended for more than forty years of service on his retirement, which the dates showed came less than a year before his death.

Connie's prescience scored again: she had rightly guessed that someone's death had given birth to Funerals.com. Jack's demise, so soon after retirement, and Lenny's decision to break out of his nine-to-five and go for the pot of gold at the end of the startup were probably not unrelated. Whatever

Jack's true interests, it was clear from Lenny's site that he saw his father as a frustrated gardener, not a happy bureaucrat.

I clicked back to Lenny's e-mail and read it again.

> You only saw my business side. There's more to me than that, and I'll get to that after Funerals.com is a great success.

No question: Lenny was his father's son, taking care of business first. In what I presumed was Lenny's wish to avoid his father's fate, he had subjected himself to the same unforgiving compromise. There's no official name for it, but given his background in insurance, Lenny might call it the "Deferred Life Plan." For the promise of full coverage under the plan, you must divide your life into two distinct parts:

Step one: Do what you have to do.
Then, eventually—
Step two: Do what you want to do.

We hear variations on this theme from childhood on: *Walk before you run. No peas, no pie. Pay your dues.* Or, perhaps in the case of Jack Dolan, as Lenny saw him, work, *then retire*—assuming you live long enough to retire—and then devote your time to your passion.

The Deferred Life Plan certainly dominates Silicon Valley. Most people think getting rich fast provides the quickest way to get past the first step—and where can you get rich faster than Silicon Valley? The problem is that, despite the undisguised affluence, the verdant hills, and media-generated mythos, the vast majority of people in Silicon Valley will not get rich. Most business ideas do not find funding. Even the majority of those that are funded—that is, vetted by very smart people who think enough of the ideas to invest in them—ultimately fail. And the lucky winners may get to step two only to find themselves aimless, directionless. Either they never knew what they "really" wanted to do or they've spent so much time in the first step and invested so much psychic capital that they're completely lost without it.

A friend of mine recently unloaded his company for a prodigious pile of cash. His share was more than $50 million. Celebrating with him in Saba, a knobby rock in the Caribbean once owned by the Dutch and now a mecca for divers, we toyed with the question of what he should do next. The only idea to consider, he insisted, was to start another business. What business? He had no clue and didn't seem to care, so long as it allowed him to measure his success by tallying the numbers. Free forever from financial worries, he could think of nothing better to do than to amass more money. This from an exceptionally bright and decent man. If, after careful consideration, he were to pursue a business he truly cared about—well, that would have been understandable—but reflexively hopping back on the carousel seemed like a waste. I could only hope that with a little more time, he would rethink things.

OF COURSE, I was in no position to criticize. If I knew anything about the Deferred Life Plan, it was because I, too, had spent years as a fully vested, card-carrying believer.

When I graduated from Brown in the mid-seventies, I had no idea what a career was or where I fit in. I tried the traditional routes and applied for internships and sent off résumés to New York. Perhaps banking or advertising, I thought. But when the bankers got a look at me, they knew I wasn't one of them and turned me down. The advertisers easily ignored my barrage of résumés. I applied to IBM—the old IBM that ran applicants through a battery of IQ and personality tests, I guess, before they even talked to you. You showed up in the morning for the tests and came back in the afternoon for interviews. When I returned after lunch, they suggested, cheerfully but firmly, that an interview wouldn't be necessary. I didn't fit the profile.

I didn't seem to fit anybody's profile. It was troublesome to me that I couldn't find a match; I had expected to settle into a career like everyone else.

In the meantime, needing a paycheck, I found a position with the city of Providence, in the Mayor's Office of Community Development. Working in city politics was fascinating. A parade of flamboyant characters marched through City Hall every day, like the back lot of some 1940s movie studio. I remember one old time politico, for instance, in charge of housing rehabilitation programs in a lower-income neighborhood, who carried a gun and sometimes brandished it at applicants whose looks he didn't like. Crazy.

Simultaneously, I also took a position teaching economics at Johnson and Wales College in the evening program. I wanted to stay in touch with economics, which was my major in college, and I liked the idea of teaching (even though home economics would probably have been a more appropriate subject matter; Johnson and Wales was best known as a cooking school). Most of my students turned out to be Vietnam vets on the GI Bill who were a good bit older than I was.

Also simultaneously, I continued to freelance for the Banzini Brothers, three music promoters, barely older than me, whom I'd met while I was on the Brown Concert Committee. Their operation delivered live performances to college campuses, small concert halls, outdoor festival grounds, and nightclubs throughout New England. After college, my role with the Brothers was hatched at a Weather Report concert.

One of them pushed me out from behind stage in my tie and jacket to head off the ASCAP police who were looking for royalty fees for cover songs. I don't remember what shuck and jive I gave them, but the copyright cops relented. I became the straight guy, the one who dealt with the unions, city hall, or rival promoters, whoever the Brothers were trying to avoid.

At times, I'd review the financial plans for upcoming concerts in order to understand how and if there was any money to be made. My compensation included free tickets to all concerts, a good table at the clubs, and an open door to the old colonial the Brothers owned near Thayer Street, at the heart of Brown's freewheeling scene. I invested all my money, which wasn't very much, in their productions. I lost it, or the majority of it, I think.

After a full day at the mayor's office and a few hours teaching, I'd head over to the Banzini Brothers headquarters for my "duties." The house attracted a constant flow of partyers, all trying to rub up against celebrity visitors and generally searching for a good time. Off to the bars or a concert until the wee hours, we kept up with our accounts—listening to bands, working the acts, recruiting fresh talent, and checking out new venues. I received an education in the way these productions were staged—how the numbers worked, the process for promoting and scheduling shows, the arrangements for talent and securing halls, all the logistics of producing concerts.

When I tell people about my experiences at that time, they often say, "It was the music, right? The other things—the mayor's office, the teaching—those paid your way, but your heart was in the rock concerts, right?"

No, I explain, my heart was in everything, in all of it together.

My Providence was this: What started as a way to fill time and pay my way while I figured out what career to pursue turned into something unexpectedly rich and fulfilling. But it wasn't any one single part of this life that excited me. It was the aggregate. All the pieces fitting together gave me satisfaction and energy. I was passionate about the whole: No one particular part attracted me to the exclusion of everything else. Each part excited me fully while I was doing it, for the moment I was doing it. My passion was for exploring everything.

I was beginning to see how creativity could thrive in the context of earning a living. With the Banzini Brothers, I helped produce concerts. They brought pleasure to people, and they were creative in the way they did it. These were kids learning the business on the fly. No one told them how to be concert promoters. They loved music, they loved events, they loved the ambience, and so they simply figured it out. Even in the mayor's office, where there was ordinarily a lot of structure, I worked on projects funded out of Washington and so new there were few precedents, little direction, and only limited guidelines. You had to start with a blank piece of paper and be creative. Even teaching turned out to be a highly creative experience. Without the benefit of formal training or guidance, I had to piece the job together in my own way.

Here was a talent, and a pleasure, I began to realize—the ability to put a blank piece of paper on the table and to create something in the context of work and business. I enjoyed sitting down, analyzing a problem, and then concocting a bunch of free-form solutions. I might have simply reinvented the wheel, made a hexagon instead of a circle, but I could get it rolling, and I wasn't afraid of venturing outside my realm of comfort and experience. A group of friends at that time, for example, started a community newspaper. I knew nothing about the newspaper business, startups, or finance.

But I took a piece of accounting paper and began to work it out—what they needed to accomplish and what it would cost. I was not only comfortable doing that, I liked it. Years later, in various Silicon Valley businesses, as I sat down to find a solution without a shred of direct experience, the thrill of Providence, that blank piece of paper, came back to me.

DESPITE MY ENERGY and passion in Providence, I held onto the notion that eventually I would need to focus my life on something "serious." Providence, I told myself, was a lark, a way of sowing my oats before settling down. Get serious, I thought. Get a profession, build a career, establish yourself, and be successful. Then you can do what you want. I was living the Deferred Life Plan.

And what was going to be my second step in the Plan, when I had paid my dues and could do what I wanted? What was it I truly wanted to do? I couldn't have articulated it at that time. In the years that followed, though, as I did build a profession and career, the Providence experience was like a casual kiss that lingered in my memory. Somehow, I thought, I wanted to recapture the essence of that life—the creativity and unbounded nature of it all.

The "serious" life I chose was the law. In the fall of 1978 I trudged off to Harvard Law School after nearly two years working in Providence. I may not have been happy at law school, but I was going somewhere. After graduation, having found some affinity for trial work when I worked summers for the San Francisco DA's office and the FTC, I became a litigator for a large Boston law firm.

I thought litigation offered the possibility of making a genuine difference in people's lives and would give me a feeling of satisfaction and purpose. Unfortunately, I soon discovered, litigation was mostly sifting through reams of paper and squabbling. Cases generally were settled before they reached the courtroom.

But not all cases. When the chance finally came to argue my first case as lead counsel, I made the most of it. One rich and important client of the firm lived on a beautiful wooded lot, and someone had cut down nineteen of his trees without permission. The firm agreed to represent him for no charge, but they assigned a junior associate—me—figuring the outcome wasn't important enough for a partner. I treated it like it was *Roe v. Wade*, working up the case with a fervor. The day the trial began, I drove an hour south of Boston to a county courthouse. The attorney for the defense was the perfect model of a country lawyer. He enjoyed an easy rapport with the judge, no doubt developed over many weekends of golfing and bonding.

Trying the case without a jury, we each made our opening statements. I argued that the defendant, a recidivist tree poacher, had knowingly entered my client's private property and destroyed nineteen trees. Furthermore, I claimed, these nineteen trees were priceless; given the timetables of nature, they were gone forever from my client's life. In taking them the defendant had maliciously invaded my client's property, land that had been in his family for generations. I asked the court for a huge judgment, which, I argued, still would not compensate the true loss to my client.

Opposing counsel admitted nothing and claimed that even if his client did cut down the trees, the act had been inadvertent. Furthermore, he held that the value of the trees was a mere twelve cents a foot or some such arcane measure, because that would be their value as lumber. Getting nowhere, the judge suggested we three retire to his chambers to discuss matters. The two old friends lit up cigars and swapped stories, hardly acknowledging my presence. Finally, the country lawyer turned toward me, "You made a good argument, kid. But I can't bring those trees back to life. My client made an honest mistake. The best calculation I've got leads me to a sum of three thousand dollars."

I was outraged. "Three thousand dollars! For what your client did!"

Unfazed, he asked whether I had visited the property.

"Yes," I said.

"A lot of trees out there, aren't there?"

"Not these nineteen any longer," I shot back.

"Who's going to miss those trees in that forest?"

"My client will. It's not a forest. It's a question of trees, and those nineteen trees were his, and now they're gone."

"Three thousand dollars is my best and final offer," he said. "We can avoid wasting your time and the judge's if you can convince your client to be reasonable."

But I'd already conferred with my client and knew he wouldn't entertain a nominal gesture. "No," I said. "My client won't accept that. It's a question of principle."

So we tried the case, and I went all out, falling over myself to right the grievous wrong done my client. The country lawyer, bemused at my performance, conducted himself like an old pro. He even helped me out a bit. When I was unsure how to introduce a piece of evidence, he was ready with advice. When I committed a procedural gaffe, he'd tell the judge he had no objection.

As the trial neared its end, I was pleased. I'd made my case and had even extracted what I thought was a vital piece of testimony from the defendant, who all but admitted on the stand that he had known where the property line was and had taken my client's trees nonetheless.

The judge retired to chambers to deliberate. I sat motionless, studiously feigning calm for my client's sake. My adversary across the aisle, meanwhile, joshed with the stenographer and inquired in concerned tones after the bailiff's family.

The judge soon reentered the courtroom and announced his verdict: "I find in favor of the plaintiff."

I won! I smiled warmly at my client, who slapped my back approvingly.

The judge continued: "I hereby order the defendant to pay to the plaintiff damages in the amount of three thousand dollars."

My smile froze. The wise, old counsel thanked the judge, shook my hand, put his arm around his client, and walked down the aisle in pleasant conversation. My heart and soul spent winning some meaningless altercation, I was left wondering whether the law was ever going to take me where I wanted to go.

In 1983 I gravitated to a newly emerging specialty, technology law, after having transferred to my law firm's Palo Alto office. Technology law concentrates on identifying, protecting, and transacting in intellectual property—ideas. It is a product of the insuppressible inventiveness of Silicon Valley. It lacked the thrill of trial work, but it was far more stimulating than the tedious rounds of discovery that dominated litigation practice.

I traded the thrust and parry of litigation for ongoing relationships with byte-sized entrepreneurs, coders. They were creating the real value in the food chain of the PC revolution: software. I became engrossed in working with these inventors, who were assembling new businesses out of Silicon Valley garage shops. They turned out to be people I could easily relate to, more like the artists the Banzini Brothers had managed in the rock and roll promotion business than like my litigation colleagues and clients. They reminded me of my passionate, offbeat high school and college friends. They were talent. I understood them. I understood their art and their art's relationship to business. And I found myself able, by dint of both my eclectic experience and my training as a lawyer, to help them build viable enterprises around their brilliant ideas.

Perhaps, I thought, I could find genuine satisfaction, some meaning, in practicing law after all.

In 1985, I approached Lucasfilm, George Lucas's film studio and the home of *Star Wars*, for some work on the sale of Pixar, its animation division, to Steve Jobs. My firm ended up handling the technology side of that deal—the conveyance of the technology, the protection of intellectual property, and so on. At that time, Pixar was hardly the distinguished company Jobs later made of it, but the transaction was still fascinating: a project with two marquee names from two glamorous worlds, entertainment and technology. I tried to take as much shine from their limelight as I could.

With negotiations completed, I orchestrated the closing, a legal ritual to seal the deal. The key people from each side attended, smiling, shaking hands, and drinking champagne. It was a happy event for everyone, it turned out, except me. I watched all those people celebrate in the boardroom, while I checked signatures and filled up boxes with documents in some stuffy little closet across the hall. It struck me that no matter how interesting the clients or the case, my work as a lawyer was extremely narrow and routine. I decided at that point I wanted to do what they were doing—write the script, not collate the pages. I wanted to be in the other room. Practicing law wouldn't put me there.

Soon after that sale was completed, people at Apple approached me about taking a position with them. While the job was in the legal department, it turned out to be largely deal making. I told the partners at my law firm about the offer, and they were horrified. They tried to persuade me that I was about to make the biggest blunder of my life. They played on my Harvard, East Coast, big-law-firm prejudices. The high art of law, they contended, was in private practice; in-house practice was a dead end. I was on the path to partnership, so I needed only to continue doing what I was doing, and the future would be rosy. Plug away, they tried to convince me, and all of it would eventually come to me.

That was the rational, analytic side of the argument, and I took it seriously. I had bought the prejudice that company lawyers were people who couldn't hack it in a good law firm. Maybe Apple was a step backwards for me. If it didn't work out, would a good law firm still take me seriously?

Yet everything in my gut told me I should go to Apple.

Those were the mid-eighties, the glory days of the company Steve Jobs had energized with ideals and values. Though he had been forced out just before I arrived, his influence still bled in five colors throughout the organization. The Apple he created was about making the power of computing accessible to everyone, about freedom from the tyranny of technology and technologists, about changing education, about using technology to help the handicapped cope with the challenges of their disabilities. While Apple clearly had to be financially successful, its more fundamental purpose was to innovate, invent, and lead an entire cultural revolution that everyone there saw leaping from those keyboards and screens with silicon brains. Apple's 1984 Super Bowl commercial, where the free thinking individual charges through the faceless, gray crowd to shatter the tyranny of Big Brother, was gospel, not hype, throughout the Apple organization. All the people I met there, passionate young people, truly believed they were changing the world, not selling computers.

I took a mental health day and rode my bicycle mile after mile through the backcountry of Marin county. Seventy-five miles later, I still didn't know what to do. The next morning, I walked into work, puzzling through the options. I can still remember sitting in my office at the end of the hall and looking down the long corridor. In a moment of clarity, I realized my whole future was in that hall, perfectly defined. From my office, I had a unobstructed view of my colleagues in their offices—the junior associates nearest, then the senior associates, the junior partners, the partners, and finally the managing partner at the far end of the hall. A neat and tidy future loomed before me. Sure, the stroll down the hallway could be reassuring and empowering in a way, but it seemed so pat, so determined. In that instant it was if I had already lived all that. Where was the blank piece of paper?

I could not put off my life any longer. I called the people at Apple and took the job.

TO: lenny@alchemy.net
FROM: randy@virtual.net
SUBJECT: A Question

Thanks for your e-mail. I truly enjoyed visiting your Web site. Your father was quite a gardener.

Deferring your life on the chance that Funerals.com will hit it big is a huge gamble. The high odds of failure don't justify betting it will buy you the freedom you want. The course of your life and the course of Funerals.com are not unrelated. Figure out what you care about and do that. If you can do it in the context of Funerals.com, do it from the start. Don't concern yourself with exit strategies.

At key points in my life, I've found it helpful to ask myself a simple question about what I was doing at that moment:

What would it take for you to be willing to spend the rest of your life on Funerals.com?

best

r
_____

Chapter Five

THE ROMANCE, NOT THE FINANCE

I WOKE EARLY TO ANOTHER BLUE, blue, cloudless California day, the sweet smell of jasmine sifting through the open windows. I grew up in upstate New York, where sunny days are not to be taken for granted, especially during the gray, dispirited days of winter. It wasn't until I headed off to college in New England that I was able to count on a few sunny days. And that was New England—not exactly a haven for sun worshippers. I started to wonder what a bit more light might do for me. Twenty years after my first trip to San Francisco, I can still remember crossing the Bay Bridge for the very first time after many days and nights on the road from Boston. I knew I was home, instantly.

I brewed a pot of green tea and sipped it in the garden, as Tali and Tika, like Keystone Cops, scampered off to chase the scent of some long-gone deer or coyote. I completed my morning rituals—meditation, the *Wall Street Journal,* and e-mail.

Lenny had already replied at 5:30 A.M. his time. I was curious if he had gone to bed at all. No wonder he'd looked tired in the Konditorei. Driven days, sleepless nights. I could empathize. I had known that exhausting combination.

TO: randy@virtual.net
FROM: lenny@alchemy.net
SUBJECT: Re: A Question

Randy,

I don't understand "do Funerals.com for the rest of my life." Nobody commits to anything forever these days. Things change too fast. Of all people, you should be the first to realize that.

But don't doubt my commitment. There's nothing I want more and nothing I won't do to make Funerals.com a success. If you have any doubts about my dedication to this venture, you can forget them. I wouldn't want you or Frank to suspect otherwise. I just need funding. I know I can make this work!

Yours,

Lenny

I never doubted Lenny's drive. It was obvious from the very beginning, even in the armlock he laid on me at the door of the Konditorei. Drive, commitment—those weren't my concern. I wanted to know what he really cared about. I wanted to know his passion. Lenny didn't seem to understand the question. He was beginning to nettle me.

The early morning traffic snarled on the only local road that led out of town to the freeway. On the motorcycle, I bobbed and weaved around the grumbling commuters, remembering an episode of the "Twilight Zone" in which the character finds himself meandering through a crowd of stone-frozen people stuck fast in the middle of their daily routines. I cut up the highway one exit, fields of golden grass on both sides, fingers of fog stretching down the pleats in the Santa Cruz Mountains to the west. I scooted across Sand Hill Road to the complex at 3000, the original Sand Hill address. No spaces, so I jumped the curb and popped the stand.

First up, I sat in on a deal pitch at one of the VC firms where some good friends wanted my opinion. The plan was to sell pet supplies on the Net. The would-be entrepreneurs called their venture PetUniverse.com.

Lenny's presentation was polished, but this one positively gleamed. Here were three guys fresh out of top-of-the-line business schools, and they *had* managed to shrink the world, or at least all pet owners, into a four-cell matrix. Their projections found the perfect balance between the aggressive and the impossible. They clearly recognized this as a "Better-Faster-Cheaper" play and understood the implications, which all boiled down to one simple dictum: execute at light speed. A herd of other aspiring Petsomethings.com startups had been making the rounds during the last month, too. Sand Hill Road was in a pet feeding frenzy, at least for the moment.

The disconcerting thing about these pet shop boys, all sharp go-getters, was that none of them, they confessed when asked, owned a pet, had ever owned a pet, or—so far as I could tell—had ever wanted to own a pet. I wouldn't have been surprised to discover they were deathly allergic to fur, feathers, and scales.

So why were they doing this? Why was it worth their time? I am always amazed that venture capitalists don't ask that question. Perhaps at this point everyone assumes it's obvious: to get rich. I tried to look at it from their perspective. Maybe this was their lark, a few years invested on the off chance that they would hit it big. Afterward they could get on with whatever was important to them. Too many times, unfortunately, I had seen this attitude lead to a lifetime of successive bets, all heading away from their original dreams. It is too easy to get lost in the hype and swallowed up by the casino economics of it all. It bothered me to see talented young people give up, or defer, their ideals in the hope of a fast buck that was unlikely to ever arrive. In considering my question, "What would make you willing . . . ," Lenny thought I was suggesting he should plan his life precisely. That's foolish. As he already pointed out, the one thing we can count on is change. But knowing what we require to be *willing* to do something life-long provides invaluable self-knowledge.

It's not, as I've learned from my own experience, that the

deferred life is just a bad bet. Its very structure—first, step one, do what you must; then, step two, do what you want—implies that what we *must* do is necessarily different from what we *want* to do. Why is that the case? In the Deferred Life Plan, the second step, the life we defer, cannot exist, does not deserve to exist, without first doing something unsatisfying. We'll get to the good stuff later. In the first step we earn, financially and psychologically, the second step. Don't misunderstand my skepticism. Sacrifice and compromise are integral parts of any life, even a life well lived. But why not do hard work because it is meaningful, not simply to get it over with in order to move on to the next thing?

The Deferred Life Plan also dictates that we divorce who we are and what we care about from what we do in that first step. By distancing the real person from her actions, all manner of bad behavior is justified in the name of business. "Sure she's an SOB at work, but that's not who she really is. It's only business, nothing personal." Fueled by ambition, we hope that in the end we will be judged by our accomplishments, not by who we are. Silicon Valley is a place where many people excuse their own behavior as "just business." I wasn't holding my breath to see the "real" them.

The distinction between drive and passion is crucial. I had asked Lenny about his *passion*. He thought I was questioning his *drive* and *commitment*. Passion and drive are not the same at all.

Passion *pulls* you toward something you cannot resist. Drive *pushes* you toward something you feel compelled or obligated to do. If you know nothing about yourself, you can't tell the difference. Once you gain a modicum of self-knowledge, you can express your passion. But it isn't just the desire to achieve some goal or payoff, and it's not about quotas or bonuses or cashing out. It's not about jumping through someone else's hoops. That's drive.

In the Deferred Life Plan, drive pushes us through the first step. The second step, the deferred life itself, is the home of passion. We hope and suppose that when we get there, we will be able to resurrect our passions on our own terms. *If* we get there.

I had passion in Providence but didn't appreciate it. I drove myself through law school and the practice of law, seeking and hoping and groping for passion but never finding it. Then in Silicon Valley—at Apple, Claris, GO, LucasArts—I discovered passion in my work. But I didn't understand the crucial difference between drive and passion until I found them at war inside me.

SOME FOUR YEARS AGO, I was CEO of Crystal Dynamics, then a three-year-old video game company. I had been recruited from LucasArts Entertainment, the province of George Lucas's empire that produced games and edutainment for the PC. Our flagship products were based on the *Star Wars* films. LucasArts was my first CEO position. It was an extremely exciting place to work, rich with talent and creativity. What prompted me to talk, however, when the headhunter called about Crystal Dynamics, was the prospect of autonomy—the ability to lead an independent company based on my vision for games and storytelling. Autonomy was supposed to have been part of the package at LucasArts, but it looked increasingly unlikely.

By mid-1995 I had become captivated by a vision of storytelling transformed by technology. For the first time, I believed, computers and their ilk would allow the audience to directly engage and interact with the story. Games represented a primitive stage in the evolution of this medium, like movies in the time of the nickelodeon. I wanted the chance to shape this new medium and contribute to its evolving grammar and vocabulary.

Crystal Dynamics had been founded to ride the wave of the much-heralded "Next Generation" video games. Crystal's titles were played on game consoles, electronic boxes that hooked up directly to TV sets. "Next Gen" game consoles ran on the then-new, more powerful 32- and 64-bit processors, which provided faster play and sharper images. They were manufactured by companies like 3DO, Nintendo, Sony, and Sega, each of which had its own unique and incompatible platform. Because most console games relied on quick reaction times, they were also known as "twitch" games, appealing mainly to adolescent boys with their muscle-bound heroes, busty women, and plenty of bloody fighting.

At first, I was troubled that Crystal's video games were toy-like in comparison with LucasArt's more cinematic PC games. But if the "Next Gen" market took off and if Crystal could achieve some early success, I believed we might be able to shift the company's focus toward interactive storytelling.

Just as I joined Crystal in May, the existing management team finished preparations for a nationwide road show to solicit a round of private investment. My first task as CEO, then, was to lead the road show, which proved a great success. Setting out to raise some $15 million, we received more than $25 million in commitments, and we accepted only $20 million at a very aggressive price. A lot for the time. Investors had liked our story.

The story we told was based on a plan prepared before I arrived. It rested on a set of assumptions about the number of products we would launch, the estimated market penetration for each, and a development timetable—all dependent on a deeper set of assumptions about the growth of the "Next Generation" console market. I hadn't had a chance to do much personal due diligence—after all, I had just arrived—but the plan seemed to hang together. In any case, we would give it our best shot, I thought, and if it didn't work, we could fix it later.

Back in the office after the road show, I began meeting with key people from the creative and sales sides of the company. We needed a detailed implementation plan to achieve the projections we had sold to investors. For weeks through late summer we gathered in marathon planning sessions, fueled by pizza and caffeine. Soon enough, alarm bells began clanging in my head. Crystal couldn't deliver on the plan. There wasn't enough pizza in the world to make it work.

This was troublesome for me in more ways than one. Investors had bought the plan, I realized, at least in part because of my track record at Lucas. It was *my* plan, and my fix-it-later attitude had been naïve. I felt responsible, and I couldn't let them down. Furthermore, I wanted very much to achieve the plan and move on to interactive storytelling, a prospect that was suddenly in great jeopardy.

The first problem was the "Next Generation" game market: How quickly would it grow and who would be the winners? The console makers manufactured the razors, and we sold blades. But for which razor? 3DO, the original "Next Generation" console platform, was floundering, and that's where Crystal had placed its first bet. Our second bet, Sega, was already off to a bad start.

The second problem was that my discussions with the creative producers raised grave doubts about their ability to develop quality titles as quickly as the plan prescribed. And if we couldn't generate enough titles, Crystal would be in trouble, even if the platforms grew as we had hoped.

Unfortunately, the weaknesses in the operating plan were only the most obvious of our problems. My probing revealed something far more serious.

Crystal was not one organization, but two. The people who made the games and the people who sold them were at war with each other. Both sides were led by equally talented management partners and staffed with strong people. Before I arrived the trenches had been dug deep. Frustrated by the vagaries of the creative process, the sales side blamed the creative side for failing to deliver on time and for not producing the games the market desired. The creative people blamed the sales people for wanting only "me-too" titles, for not being able to effectively sell potential hits, and for goading them into foolishly aggressive development schedules.

As summer ended, I could see that we had an unworkable plan *and* an internecine war, but the prospect of failure never occurred to me. As colleagues warned that the sky was falling, I quickly reassured them that we would be fine, that I had seen worse, much worse.

In truth, I understood the company's most basic problem and knew what to do about it: In its initial zeal to become a major player, Crystal had tried to instantly become a full-service developer and publisher with its own sales and distribution resources, even before it had produced a reliable pipeline of successful products. A sales force requires a steady flow of marketable titles to sustain itself, and Crystal wasn't capable of delivering them yet. Crystal had tried to do too much too fast.

My instincts, reinforced by my experience at LucasArts, said we should take a step backward and do this right: Cut back the sales side of the business, and retreat to the core of the company—the creative organization. Focus all our resources on developing a small number of high-quality games. Sell these games through outside publishers. Then, when we had a stable of successful titles, rebuild Crystal's own sales organization, and recapture the control and margin given up to the distribution partners. We would likely wind up in the same place sought by the founders, but by a different route and with less risk at each step.

Naturally, the prospect of pulling back from the plan did not excite the board. The success of the road show was still a vivid memory, and hope among many of the board members of achieving the original dream—quickly becoming a dominant, publicly traded, full-service developer and publisher of "Next Generation" games—remained high, despite management's growing doubts.

Instead of pressing for what I believed in the face of their resistance, I offered two alternatives. Scale up by acquiring other companies and creative teams. Or sell out. If Crystal Dynamics could find a company that would value our people, our products, and our early position in the market we could avoid layoffs and still give the investors a good return. Moreover, I would be free of my dilemma.

For the next few months, we considered candidates for purchase and held discussions with a number of them, but we never found an acquisition that made sense. At the same time, through that winter, we looked high and low for another company to acquire us. We held serious discussions with more than one potential buyer, but those came to nothing and only confirmed my worst fears: as the game business consolidated, the buyers preferred companies with far more revenue and better-established products than we had.

The board's reaction to my alternatives also proved to be divided. A majority opposed selling because their hearts remained set on building a successful independent company. There was no consensus either that we should grow by acquisition, even if we could find good candidates, because of the inevitable dilution to the investors. In something of a precursor to the Internet "premature IPO" phenomenon, some board members even suggested going public, but I couldn't see how that would solve our operating problems and refused to support it. We needed to get our house in order first. January and February came and went, and we were still trapped by disagreement and indecision.

So began my sleepless nights. They were not sleepless because of the business problems—serious as those were, I had faced worse in other companies without losing sleep— but because I began to recognize a fundamental flaw in my relationship with the company.

If I understood the problem and the solution, why didn't I act on it? Why didn't I shut down the sales organization? I had stood up to resistant board members on other issues— why not now, on the most important issue of all?

Resolution for me and for the company did not come until May, a year after I joined Crystal. That month the Electronic Entertainment Expo, the industry's annual trade show, known as E3, was held in Los Angeles. Hollywood had become enamored with the game business, and they were going to up the ante with their star power and cachet.

What did not bode well for Crystal was obvious as I surveyed the exhibit hall: several game publishers—glitzed out with dancing showgirls, pinups signing autographs, and huge screens featuring the latest releases—dwarfed my little company. We had puffed up to look like a substantial player for the show, but we seemed puny by comparison. And we were running out of time.

One evening, I cruised the industry parties with Toni, a friend of mine. A very bright and exotic woman, part French, part American Indian, with a strong aesthetic sense, Toni had cofounded a game company that made cool, avant-garde games for the PC. Her titles weren't best-sellers, but they were beautiful and innovative, and, not surprisingly, she was not a fan of Crystal's shoot-'em-ups and fantasy play.

As we whizzed along the freeway in a limo, each of us half drunk, she turned to me rather suddenly. "What are you doing in the game business?" The way she said it was "the *game* business." What are you doing in the *game* business?

Taking her challenge, I sobered up enough to launch into my grand vision speech: We're at an early stage, but it's the dawn of a new era of entertainment and storytelling. . . . We're learning to put together the pieces and developing the vocabulary. . . . Yada, yada, yada.

She listened politely to my entire spiel. But when I finished, she crossed her arms over her chest and maintained matter-of-factly, "You're in the fucking game business."

Her words jolted me like a hammer to my not-so-sober head.

I hardly played games as a kid. I'd never played a video game all the way through. There always seemed to be something more important to do. I liked sports, because there was beauty in physical prowess. But games to me always seemed a distraction. I was definitely not a gamer.

I sighed, sinking into the plush seats, a weight suddenly off my shoulders. "I'm in the *game* business," I confessed—to myself as much as to Toni.

I had joined Crystal with a vision of taking the company

to a new level of interactive, cinematic entertainment, but the prospects for achieving that had evaporated months earlier. Cutting back the company would have meant confronting what I already realized but couldn't admit: Crystal was going to be a video game company, plain and simple, nothing more. My *drive* said, "Stay and make it work," while my *passion* prevented me from making the changes needed to do so.

The next Monday, I returned to the office and called in my two lieutenants. I explained what they already knew, that Crystal Dynamics was trying to do too much. Given the size of our competitors, we would bleed to death if we didn't change course. We had to shrink the company, I continued, to its core strengths. Naturally they were uncomfortable with my decision, even though they had long been frustrated with my inaction. I asked them to suggest strategies for carrying out the reorganization, and they went off to ponder the options.

Next I met with two key board members and told them my decision. We had skirted this issue more than once without conclusion, but this time there had to be resolution. So I added something further: I was resigning. I would stay long enough to help the company scale back, but I wouldn't run it any more. What was right for Crystal wasn't right for me.

In the end, my two lieutenants, whose groups had fought so bitterly with each other, resigned as well. One of the board members stepped in to lead a scaled back Crystal focused on producing a few quality games that were distributed by larger players. Crystal was finally sold two years later, a small video game company gobbled up by a larger video game company.

My departure created turmoil and bitterness for many involved. I felt I had done the unforgivable. I had bailed out of a plane that was still in midair. Yet when I finally asked myself the question that I had encouraged Lenny to ask himself, I could not ignore the chasm between my own passion and what the company needed. Without a grander vision, and some prospect of realizing it, Crystal was not a place I could see myself working the rest of my life. That meant I needed to get out, now.

My MIND came back to the PetUniverse.com pitch. At least, I thought, I'd started at Crystal with a story and a passion. All I saw in this pitch was greed.

I had begun to find aspects of the startup game increasingly disturbing. Expedience ruled. Sometimes I wondered if, rather than developing tomorrow's business leaders and talent, we weren't merely cloning speculators, hack business men and women, who arbitraged their drive for a quick hit and who believed that if you're rich, you're right. Heaven help us if these businesses actually have to be operated on a bottom line basis for the long run.

I retreated to my home and checked my messages. After the kind of morning I had, I felt compelled to e-mail Lenny.

The deferred life: drive, then passion.

Who wants that?

```
TO: Lenny@alchemy.net
FROM: randy@virtual.net
SUBJECT: Ask it again

Lenny,

You completely missed the point of my
question.

It's not about doing the same job for
life. It's about what things you would
```

consider worth doing ~~today if it were~~
your last day.

Don't confuse drive and passion. Drive
pushes you forward. It's a duty, an
obligation. Passion pulls you. It's the
sense of connection you feel when the
work you do expresses who you are. Only
passion will get you through the tough
times.

As I tell the M.B.A. classes I sometimes address, it's the romance, not
the finance that makes business worth
pursuing.

You need something in Funerals.com that
by itself will inspire you, and others
with you, to prevail, no matter what
adversity arises. In my experience, the
promise or hope of money by itself
won't do.

Ask yourself the question again.

best

r

Chapter Six

THE BIG IDEA

THE NEXT MORNING I headed toward San Jose for a board meeting. Traveling south on Highway 280 offers none of the gleaming lakes and plush hills that texture the landscape leading to San Francisco. After a brief stretch of road flanked by Stanford's rolling open spaces, grazed by meandering cows, and spotted with giant radio telescope dishes, sprawl displaces the more bucolic scenery. First, suburbia with its housing developments and strip malls. Then block after block crammed with one- and two-story buildings whose fronts are stamped with a veneer of business respectability but whose three other sides drop the pretense. "Tilt ups," built in a hurry to house wave after wave of new industries, these generic cubes have replaced boundless acres of cherry, plum, and apricot orchards. This is the "silicon" in Silicon Valley, the place where the Fairchilds, Intels, and their progeny were born. Microprocessing plants, chip fabs, clean rooms full of drab bunny suits; this is the place. Like a ghetto that takes on the face of each new wave of immigrants, this part of the Valley has, in turn, sheltered the chip, computer, software, and now Internet hopefuls. In the future, anthropologists will be able to identify each generation of the Valley's industries by sifting through the flotsam and jetsam of endless remodels. A sudden rash of competitors marks each industry cycle; then the industry peaks and consolidates into a handful of winners. In no time another wave of wannabe industry-builders moves in and fills the vacancies. It's "recycling," Valley style.

I made haste to the offices of TiVo, a high flyer with a big idea, attracting a lot of attention with its promise of changing the entertainment world. The conference room hummed with activity this morning. Various VCs and industry leaders in their denim and khaki finery milled and munched pastries and bagels, clustered in twos and threes. Meanwhile, the management team welcomed arriving board members. Mike Ramsey, CEO and one-half of the founding team, was dressed in the stylish LA banded-collar, pleated-slacks look. In his late forties, Mike's dignified gray is unusual in startups these days. He is an experienced leader, poised and polished and always appreciative of the people who work with him. His sidekick and co-founder, Jim Barton, on the cusp of forty and dressed in jeans and a button-down shirt, looks like he grew up on the range. A no-nonsense technologist, he always gives it to you straight. The rest of the executive team, attired somewhere along the Mike-Jim continuum, excused themselves from the room periodically to deal with whatever momentary emergency required their attention. The finely tailored director from New York, in a blue suit and white shirt that Lenny would have appreciated, stood a little off to the side, pouring himself another cup of coffee and adding a generous splash of milk.

The room was decorated, if that's the right word to use, in the mode of "Valley professional": stark, functional, disdaining extravagance. A wood conference table for a dozen or more dominated the space. A sleek black box the size of a large laptop computer carefully perched atop a television set somewhat inconspicuously in the far corner. Except for the parking lot, where the shiny, late-model luxury cars attested to many earlier wins, it was hard to tell that the assembled group comprised some of the Valley's most prominent deal makers and game changers.

In these early-stage businesses, where progress is measured in minutes, monthly board meetings are the norm. At this moment, TiVo was only two years old, and it had already raised more than $100 million, attracting an illustrious group of investment partners, including Sony, AOL, Disney, DIRECTV, Philips, CBS, NBC, Liberty Media, TV Guide, Showtime, and Quantum. It had launched a world-class product and service, and it had assembled a stellar team.

Now TiVo was on the verge of what most founders think of as Heaven. It was about to go public. Looking around the room, though, I would say exhaustion trumped elation. And unlike Lenny and other wannabes like him, these guys viewed an IPO as a means, not an end—as a financial pit stop, a chance to refuel for the long—the very long—road ahead.

TiVo had attracted such high-profile support because of its unusual potential—because of the power of the idea and the promise of fundamental change. I had first heard of the company in the autumn of 1997, when Stewart Alsop, a Silicon Valley pundit, columnist, and venture capitalist partner in New Enterprise Associates, called me about the initial idea. He and Geoff Yang, a prominent venture capitalist then at Institutional Venture Partners and now at Redpoint Ventures, were seeding a startup called Teleworld, TiVo's first incarnation. A few days later I headed over to the Konditorei to listen to the founders' pitch. Mike Ramsey was a distinguished executive from Silicon Graphics, where he had run a large piece of the business, and Jim Barton was a standout engineering wizard who had also come from SGI. Among those who pitch me, they were unusual in their maturity and accomplishments. SGI had been involved with Time Warner Cable's video-on-demand trials in Orlando, Florida. An ambitious attempt to cost effectively deliver to home viewers a vast library of movies they could watch at their convenience, those trials had been a bust, but Mike and Jim wanted to apply the lessons learned to a new venture.

Their Teleworld idea was to sell a new kind of hardware, a home server that not only digitally stored incoming electronic information, including audio and video content, but also linked the gamut of digital devices rapidly becoming commonplace in the home: computers, PDAs, and Internet appliances. Concerned that they might be ahead of the market and that customers would be slow to appreciate the ultimate value of their product, Mike and Jim planned to jump-start the business by giving customers the ability to digitize and store several hours of television programming in a set-top box. Their initial product would be, in effect, a souped up VCR with a clever programming guide. Because of the costly electronic storage requirements, it would carry a hefty price tag.

Their strategy made me cringe. Working at companies like GO and WebTV convinced me that there is no margin in the consumer hardware business. It requires an enormous investment, demands massive distribution, and scales slowly. I believed the value of consumer hardware could be derived only from the services it delivered to the consumer and industry partners (in this case, advertisers, programmers, and networks). The business model inherent in such a strategy, though, is uncertain. If you price the hardware high enough to generate acceptable margins, your product's retail price is too costly to quickly develop the volume of users needed to enable a robust service business. On the other hand, unlike with Internet services and software where there is no or nominal marginal expense for each new user, the cost of subsidizing these pricey boxes to make them affordable in order to accelerate adoption could break the bank. Mike and Jim talked about selling hundreds of thousands of set-top boxes, but that wouldn't build a large enough audience for service providers and advertisers. They would have to sell millions of units, and quickly. If they focused on the boxes, I told them, "your legacy may be that you sowed the seeds of a huge market, which the consumer electronics giants and service providers ultimately reaped." Pioneer new territory, I cautioned, but don't end up with arrows in your backs.

What a buzzkill I was. They were gracious and thanked me for my candor. As we parted, I couldn't imagine how they would succeed in the hardware business they envisioned, and I never expected to hear from them again. Entrepreneurs, in my experience, don't like to be told they're wrong. It isn't in their dispositions to sit and listen to that kind of critique. That's why many ideas in this Valley happen against all common sense. It's good when entrepreneurs are a little bit deaf and blind, but if they're completely deaf and completely blind—and many are—they're unlikely to learn enough from the market and their advisors to make their vision a reality.

To my surprise, Mike called back a week later, and I agreed to meet again. He and Jim hadn't taken my advice wholesale, but they had carefully considered it and revised their plans where they thought their ideas could be improved. Their new idea, which ultimately became TiVo, was much, much bigger.

In essence, they had evolved the business from a hardware-based model to a service-based strategy. The gist of their big idea was what they called "personalized television." Using the box and its ability to record programming, they now proposed to build a service that would give viewers complete, individualized control over what they viewed on television and when they viewed it. They would price the box lower to foster sales in higher volume, leaping into a financial no-man's-land in a gamble that they could assemble a marketable audience in time for the service revenues to kick in and more than compensate for their losses on the boxes. How would they make money when each box was priced below cost? Volume—that is, a volume of viewers sufficient to fund a money-making service based on subscriptions, advertising, and commerce. The mix among those revenue sources and the balance between how much would come from consumers and how much would come from industry partners would be determined later. Eventually they believed that the stand-alone hardware and its expense would disappear as televisions and other set-top boxes provided the power and digital storage necessary for personalized television. Then TiVo would be a service provider only, with a much stronger financial model.

I listened to their new idea and realized that if they succeeded, the grid between television programming and network time slots would be broken. If the viewer was watching a show that had been time-shifted, commercials would no longer have a captive audience. The viewer could simply skip forward at will. He could watch a show broadcast Sunday mornings during weekday prime time, and vice versa. Advertisers who paid top dollar for prime-time audiences might or might not reach those audiences any more. With TiVo's box, your time was prime time, anytime you watched. Control would move from the broadcast networks to every single member of the audience. Television would never be the same.

There was more, I realized, because TiVo would be interactive. The service required a phone connection for data transmission and customer support, which created a direct path to and from every single viewer. Viewers would be able to communicate with the TiVo service for a myriad of purposes—at first to express opinions about shows or organize their own lineups and, eventually, if anyone cared, to buy the blouse right off an actress's back. As you watched television, your box would learn what you liked and, if you wanted, automatically find and save it for you. Eventually you would receive only relevant advertising and marketing messages, targeted to your interests. These services depended on sophisticated technology at the back end, but users wouldn't have to know about any of that. It would all be transparent to them.

This was a chance to find value in increasingly segmented audiences. An audience of two million might be worth more than an audience of twenty million, because of what was known about those two million people. Better to send an advertisement for Corvettes to a small audience composed entirely of affluent single males than to a large audience composed mostly of working couples with three kids. Best of all, the audiences' personal profiles would be private and secure, allowing viewers to decide when and if they wanted to share personal information. The possibilities raised by this vision were enormous, but many pieces would need to come together to make it work, and many incumbents in the television business might see the impending changes as a threat and resist.

As I sat in the Konditorei during that second meeting with Mike and Jim, my mind was spinning through the possibilities. I thought, "These guys don't need $20 million, they need $200 million just for starters." This effort would require experienced leaders, a management team capable of forging a complex set of relationships among advertisers, programmers, broadcasters, and content creators. The team risked making enemies of those behemoths unless they could convince them to join the movement. The incumbents could not be ignored, because their roles in the future of television entertainment would remain critical. It all depended on content, and somebody, somewhere, would have to pay for it. It was unlikely that everything would become pay-per-view, and so the role of advertisers would remain powerful, and then both content and advertising would still need to be distributed by networks and broadcasters. This would require shuttle diplomacy, not simply technological prowess.

I couldn't resist their big idea. When they invited me to help make it a reality, I didn't hesitate. Eventually I joined the executive committee of the board of directors.

For two years, Mike and Jim tirelessly evangelized the industry players, and after their initial alarm, the leaders were intrigued enough by this big idea to offer support. Now TiVo needed to raise a large sum in order to finance its race to roll out the technology and build an audience. It was time to go to Wall Street. We were at today's board meeting to bless this next step, the IPO.

Much of the meeting focused on Byzantine legal issues regarding an initial offering. The lawyers from Cooley Godward, a venerable Valley firm, reviewed the status of the Red Herring, an initial filing with the SEC. Most of us had heard the litany before, so the lawyers balanced doing their duty with being succinct. They discussed the accounting issues regarding stock options granted to employees. The SEC claimed that some of these were priced below market. If the federal watchdog only knew how hit or miss these ventures were, how sudden the surge forward toward an IPO could come on, they might better understand why almost every company in the Valley regularly faced the "cheap stock" issue. The lawyers cautioned us against discussing the IPO during the "quiet period," another faux pas, according to the SEC, because it can be misconstrued as prematurely promoting the stock. We were reminded, as was common practice with IPOs, that the company's employees and investors would be "locked up," or forbidden from trading in TiVo stock, for 180 days, thus ensuring a more manageable stock price in the six months following the offering. Finally, the SEC wanted clarification about my title, "Virtual CEO," and asked that it be changed to avoid misleading the market. Old dogs don't take well to new tricks, and it was once again obvious why the new economy germinated in the Valley.

The board cautioned the management team to avoid becoming too distracted or euphoric about the IPO. Not even founders and management committed for the long haul can avoid some preoccupation with the IPO's life-changing potential. The first day of trading can be mesmerizing for those who have worked tirelessly to build the company. To these entrepreneurs, the IPO is proof they aren't lunatics. They are finally able, at least temporarily, to stop protesting to family and friends that this work will make a difference and that they are sane despite having sacrificed everything for this chance. After the IPO, riding the share price around the curves and corners can make you dizzy. Good management must remind people constantly to ignore the jerking and lurching of the market and focus on the horizon. Stay.com.

TiVo had a chance to change the status quo for the better, with a potential we could only guess at. Sure, the market and business model were not yet proven, the incumbents could stonewall, and competitors large and small might hijack the opportunity, but Mike and Jim were up for the challenge: smart, experienced, flexible, capable of learning on the fly, and willing to do what it would take to win. They did not waste any time speaking to me about exit strategies. Personalized television would be their legacy.

I returned home midafternoon, changed into shorts and a T-shirt, opened the doors to the hills, let the dogs mosey a bit, and spent an hour or so working out in the downstairs exercise-room-cum-office-cum-dog-dorm. I lifted a few weights and put in some time on the treadmill while taking and responding to phone messages, my own recipe for multitasking. Then I checked e-mails. Surprise, surprise. Lenny had not disappeared. Tucked in the middle of several messages was one marked "Urgent!"

TO: randy@virtual.net
FROM: lenny@alchemy.net
SUBJECT: Pay Dirt

Hey Randy,

Great news!

Frank called and wants us to present next Monday morning at his partners' meeting. This is the break we've been waiting for. I don't know what you said, but thank you.

One little glitch. Allison, my partner, got a job offer she's considering taking. I think she's losing patience—just when all our work is beginning to pay off! The job offer is from some HMO. She'd be involved with developing a strategy for supporting members on the Net, though it doesn't compare to Funerals.com. She's agreed to come with me for the presentation Monday, but she's wavering between Funerals.com and the new job.

Would you be willing to get together with us after we meet with Frank and his partners? If Allison had the chance to talk with you, I have a feeling she'd be back on board, especially if the meeting with Frank goes well. I realize you don't know her, so I'm forwarding her e-mail along with another revised version of the business plan.

I've given a lot of thought to your question, but right now I need to focus on the meeting.

I can almost smell the money! Finally--
I can't believe it.

Lenny

I let out a sigh. Stranger things have happened. As any other good VC would do, Frank was sniffing around that big market, and Lenny was his only play for the moment. I'm sure that as soon as he heard from Frank, Lenny eagerly set aside all the issues I was raising. Why bother with some loopy metaphysical question if you're going to raise the money anyway and get rich in the process?

Allison's indecision posed a critical challenge to Lenny. If he lost her, it would be a serious blow to his chances. I opened her e-mail.

TO: lenny@alchemy.net
FROM: "Allison Whitlock" awhitlock@digger
.net
SUBJECT: Re: California Here We Come!!

Hi, Lenny,

All right, I'll go. I don't want you to
fail, even if I'm not associated with
Funerals.com in the long run. You have
labored so hard for this. Whatever happens, I hope it works out for you. You
deserve it.

But please understand, even if I go
with you, I am not committing. I'm having trouble seeing in Funerals.com now
the idea that attracted me to it in the

first place. When we started talking
about it and planning for it, when you
and your family were having such a hard
time with your dad's death, we saw it
as a way to help people who are struggling with loss and grief. It wasn't
just selling cheaper caskets. As you
say, that's a good place to start, and
I understand why investors will focus
on the economics of the business. But
personally? I'm not interested in simply being an e-tailer.

I'll help as much as I can. But I'm not
there yet. I have to let the HMO know
in ten days.

Later,

Al

It wouldn't have surprised me if Lenny's partner bailed out because she'd received a better offer, something concrete in contrast to the hazard inherent in a startup. But I hadn't considered that she might be at odds with Lenny's lifeless mission or that their original idea might have been more compassionate and compelling than Lenny now let on. I couldn't tell from the little Allison said, but "helping people who are struggling with loss and grief" seemed more intriguing to me than flogging cheaper caskets. A bigger idea. I was already beginning to like this Allison.

The chance to work on a big idea is a powerful reason for people to be passionate and committed. The big idea is the glue that connects with their passion and binds them to the mission of an organization. For people to be great, to accomplish the impossible, they need inspiration more than financial incentive. Lenny appeared to be jettisoning his founding vision for some misguided notion of what success demanded. He was trying to reduce Funerals.com to an equation, a formula, a model. Impatience wasn't Allison's problem. Finding something in Funerals.com to care about was.

HER AMBIVALENCE and Lenny's focus on the formula over the mission brought to mind my experience at Apple, specifically one of the most pivotal negotiations I was involved in there, which was reported only recently for the first time.

Apple's big idea had been Computing for the Rest of Us. But the company increasingly found itself hostage to the margins and quarterly results generated by its business model, which was built around premium hardware. Its share of the PC business was limited as it became addicted to selling computers at much higher margins and prices than its competition. Its intuitive, friendly interface was the justification for those margins, but that business model and Apple's position were threatened by none other than Microsoft. In 1986 we had all seen Windows 1.0, and while it posed no threat to the Macintosh operating environment at the time, we understood what it meant. Microsoft's toe, even its whole foot, was in the water. At some point it would develop a product that was good enough. Then the competition would look sufficiently like Apple to erode Apple's margins and back it into a corner of its own making, with declining share and profit.

Along with many others inside Apple, I was a strong proponent of licensing the Macintosh operating system in order to preempt Microsoft in setting the standard for user-friendly computing. After all, it was Apple's birthright, its overriding mission. It would mean cannibalizing our own model, sacrificing margins for volume and market share, but it seemed better than circling the wagons and defending an ever-declining piece of the PC business. Apple's general counsel, my boss, asked me to develop a licensing plan for the Mac operating system, with safeguards for protecting Apple's basic interests.

In a first step toward a new strategy, a colleague and I were assigned to negotiate a license of the Mac look and feel to Apollo Computer in Massachusetts, one of the leading manufacturers of workstations at the time. My partner, Mike Homer, was a prodigy in Apple's marketing organization. He was facile with technology and had a flair for sales and marketing. Later he would play a crucial role at Netscape. The two of us tag-teamed the negotiations with Apollo for months, flying back and forth across the country, coordinating with the mother ship in Cupertino, and eventually reaching an agreement.

Now all we needed was the signature of John Sculley. Mike brought the agreement to Apple's executive staff, fully expecting it to be signed and the company to announce it was finally licensing the operating system to others. Negotiating the deal had been a deliberate process, the outcome of a calculated strategy for which there had been something of a consensus. What happened instead—typical Apple management style at the time—was that pent-up reservations about our margins and business model surfaced and carried the day. Sculley caved in at the eleventh hour. We barely managed to catch the Apollo people, en route to Cupertino for the final signing and celebration, at Logan Airport in Boston.

The news was more than an embarrassment. Arguably, refusing to license the Mac OS was a fatal mistake for Sculley and his management team, and a critical misstep for Apple. No one could know what might have happened if Apple had gone ahead with that agreement and with licensing the operating system to other manufacturers.

Sculley's Apple subordinated the company's big idea to the business model. That model was not the essence of Apple. It was simply that moment's best means of realizing value from the big idea. The business model can and should change over time, as the world changes. Ultimately, when the big idea was lost, the market and Apple's employees could no longer find a reason to support Apple's business. Their fanaticism faded to ambivalence.

I was curious about whether Lenny was following the example of Sculley's Apple even before he'd been able to start the business. Was he selling the business model rather than the big idea—whatever it was—that had attracted Allison and him to Funerals.com in the beginning?

Business conditions are forever changing. You need to reconsider your strategies and business models constantly and adjust them where necessary. But the big idea that your company pursues is the touchstone for these refinements. Ditching the big idea in order to deal with business exigencies leaves you without a compass. I always advise companies to define their business in terms of where it's going, what it's becoming, not simply where it is. Set the compass, then work hard to clear a path, knowing that you may meander as you stumble upon obstacles but will always keep heading toward the same coordinates.

I sent Lenny an e-mail confirming that I looked forward to meeting him and Allison next Monday and went outside to pester the dogs.

Chapter Seven

THE
BOTTOM
LINE

"ONE MEGA, double, decaf, nonfat latte, please."

"Oh, a *Why Bother?*" Connie winked at me. "You do live dangerously."

I handed her my $2.49 and headed to my usual table just outside the door. Why bother, I thought, with a drink that has so little soul, that looks like the real thing, but that has lost its punch through some tedious processing. The portions keep getting larger, but the zest has been replaced with a faint trace. Perhaps it was time to return to drip.

I took a sip of hot foam and hoped for something more satisfying from Lenny's revised business plan, version 8.0, which

I put on the table in front of me. I'd arrived early to spend a few minutes reviewing it. If Lenny's claims were true, this version answered all the nagging questions and set Funerals.com on the path to greatness.

I glanced through it. He had reworked the market and share estimates to more aggressively dominate a slightly smaller market. He had added a section explaining how he'd find prospects, primarily through referrals from healthcare professionals who work with the dying and survivors. He had even prepared an organizational chart, with himself as CEO and Allison as VP of marketing. The rest of the boxes were blank. Including Allison in the plan was Lenny's wishful thinking. All in all, he had made a few tactical improvements, but it was still "Better-Faster-Cheaper" caskets. Lenny was prepared to try, it seemed, to squeak by in his presentation. I wondered how Frank and his partners would react.

I looked up to see Lenny and a woman who had to be Allison walking across the parking lot. Far taller than Lenny, Allison seemed to take one stride to his two. Lenny was gesticulating, nearly hopping with excitement as they approached. Allison smiled as Lenny pointed me out, said something, and laughed. An inside joke I'd have to suss out later. The VC meeting must have gone well.

"Randy, it couldn't have gone better!" Lenny bellowed when he was nearly upon me. As he reached for my hand, he added, "Frank was great. He pulled for us. I feel really good about this."

No armlock this time. Instead he patted me on the shoulder. We were buddies now. "Thanks to you, Randy."

Yeah, right.

He introduced Allison as his "partner."

"You two want something to drink?" he said. "On me."

I pointed at the half-full cup before me. Don't get me started again, I thought. Lenny went off to the counter.

Allison and I shook hands, and she pulled a white plastic chair from the adjoining table and sat down.

"So it went pretty well?" I asked her, trying to conceal my concerns.

"I think so," she said. "Lenny's very pleased." If there was a hint of doubt in her voice, she was carefully masking it.

Dressed conservatively in a dark suit and white blouse with a navy scarf, Allison kept her hair pulled back modestly from her face. She and Lenny made a matched pair. But the similarity ended there. With her height and bearing, Allison's quiet confidence was the antithesis of Lenny's edgy energy. I would be surprised, I thought, if she were the spin machine he was. At the moment, in her look and manner, she seemed reserved, or perhaps just reflective. She probably hadn't known what to expect when she agreed to accompany Lenny for this meeting.

"What happened?" I persisted. "What did Frank say?"

"He seemed very positive when he walked us out at the end. He promised he'd be in touch."

Well, he's a man of his word, but his graciousness did not tell me anything.

I watched Lenny at the counter, entertaining Connie. He was no doubt regaling her with news of the meeting and prophecizing a big check. She was practicing her active listening.

Notwithstanding their happy smiles, both Lenny and Allison actually looked spent from their morning. As these events go, they were probably only one of several auditioning teams on the roster at Frank's firm. The partners usually sit around an enormous, wooden conference table equipped with every space-age audio-video device known to man. Of course, no

one ever knows how to use it all, and no matter how techni-
cally distinguished the founders, it always seems an eternity
as the last-minute technical glitches are wrestled to the
ground before the pyrotechnics begin. Eager young assis-
tants enter at will, passing scraps of paper to partners. Partners leave, and new ones enter. As a presenter, you hope all
this coming and going involves intrigues of dramatic proportions, but it usually means something more innocent—a
partner's new Mercedes has arrived or arrangements need
to be made to pick up the kids after school. In spite of the
informality, the whole experience leaves many presenting
teams feeling stripped naked. Sometimes a team never even
proceeds beyond the first slide, as the inquisitors hurl unan-
swerable or painfully sensitive questions that cut through
dreams with surgical precision. I have observed the ritual
many times. Every day, in the lobbies of Sand Hill Road,
scores of founders sit nervously waiting their turn with the
dentist.

"Sounds like you sailed through without a problem," I
probed.

"Oh, I wouldn't say that," she replied. "I don't know how
these things are supposed to go, but there were lots of tough
questions. They seemed tough to me, anyway. I'm not sure we
answered to their satisfaction, but Lenny seems to think so."

Lenny returned with Allison's black tea and his coffee.

I changed the topic. "Lenny never told me," I said to Allison, "how you and he got together on Funerals.com."

She smiled, more relaxed with this tack. "We've known
each other most of our lives."

They played together as kids. She had been born in Boston,
but her parents moved shortly after to the Midwest. Times
were hard, so she spent summers with her grandmother, who

lived next door to Lenny and his family. Somehow Lenny and she became fast friends. She was a few years older than he.

"We lost touch when I stopped visiting," she said. "We only ran into each other again eight or ten months ago."

Allison, back in Boston for her grandmother's seventy-fifth birthday, learned that Lenny's father had died suddenly that week. The next day she attended the funeral and paid her respects. Afterward, she and Lenny fell into talking about the funeral and the complications caused by the fact that Jack's children, not to mention his many brothers and sisters, were scattered around the country. Lenny and Allison's discussions turned into exchanges of lengthy e-mails and then face-to-face meetings as they laid the plans for Funerals.com.

Allison, who held a master's degree in social work and had worked her way up over the course of eight years to head of marketing for a chain of funeral homes, knew the industry. Her knowledge and Lenny's fascination with the Internet formed the impetus for Funerals.com.

"Lenny's the salesman here," she added. "He's had to carry all the water with the business plans and presentations."

I asked Lenny, "Did you give them your funeral home pitch today?"

He shook his head a bit sheepishly.

"I told him I'd walk out if he did," Allison laughed.

"Tell me what you thought about the meeting, Lenny," I said.

"Meeting with you and working through your questions," he began, "was like practicing for today's presentation, the main event. All the detail about markets and distribution went over just great."

He went on to recount the meeting blow by blow, as Allison sat quietly. He had talked through his slides. There were many questions, he said, about the market and about how the funeral business worked now. They answered all the questions, and Allison and her knowledge of the business were invaluable. Frank was extremely helpful. He made sure key points were brought out and understood. Like Allison, Lenny put great stock in Frank's manner and words as he politely walked them out.

It was a mystery to me. The way Lenny described it, the presentation sounded like a lovefest. I began to wonder what Frank and his partners were putting in their own coffee. This didn't sound like your run of the mill VC presentation. Nor did it sound like the meeting Allison had started to describe moments earlier.

"And the tough questions?" I wondered.

"There were some tough questions now and then," Lenny said, "but nothing we couldn't handle. I think everybody was happy with the answers."

Allison's brow creased. "Frank was supportive," she finally offered. "And they do seem genuinely interested in the market. I don't think they hear many ideas like this. I mean, I can't imagine too many hot, young Internet entrepreneurs are dying to work in the funeral business."

Lenny laughed.

"But, Lenny, I thought Phil asked some questions we didn't fully address," she said. She watched Lenny, knowing that she was contradicting him.

I knew Phil, one of Frank's partners—he's a wiry, intense, former academic noted for wearing suspenders and bow ties. He had taught engineering at Stanford before becoming a VC. "I think we handled them all right," Lenny defended.

"But I was watching him closely while you were talking, and I don't know if he was . . ."

"Yeah, but Frank covered for us," Lenny cut her off. "He'll take care of it. He was very upbeat at the end."

"What did Phil say?" I asked, looking at Allison this time.

"Well," she said. "He wanted to know how many people were going to buy our products on-line. He was skeptical that people would be so deliberate at such an emotional time. Would they shop around? Why would they use the Web to research their choices? Lots of questions like that." She stopped for a moment. "I don't think he was satisfied. Phil stopped taking notes and started doodling long before Lenny was done," she remembered.

This sounded more like the meetings I was familiar with.

"But Phil was the only skeptic," Lenny said, "out of the whole group."

I told him I doubted that. Most VCs require unanimity among partners before they move forward with a deal. They won't invest unless they all agree, or close to it. In these meetings, there's usually a proponent for each idea. Frank brought Lenny in, so he was probably playing the role of good cop. He made sure all the points in favor of the idea got presented, were understood, and were discussed. VCs want to run prospects through their paces, but it makes no sense to crucify them. So there's a good cop, and often some other partner will assume the role of bad cop to ask the hard questions and probe the issues that surfaced in earlier discussions among the partners. Sounds like Phil was the bad cop this morning. He may have been the one asking the tough questions, but he was probably speaking for all the partners, even Frank, in his skepticism.

"You may have been so busy presenting that you missed the signals," I suggested to Lenny.

Lenny looked at me for a moment, miffed. "You had to be there," he finally said.

And I wasn't. True enough.

"Phil was most worried," Allison went on, "that if we pioneer the market, some big funeral chain, like my company, would see the opportunity and decide to compete with us. They have the size and money we don't have, and their network of local funeral homes is a big advantage."

"But they're slow and stuck in their old business model," Lenny pushed back. "They have to support all that brick and mortar with high margins. That's what I said in the meeting. They won't cannibalize their current business. Besides, when the brick-and-mortar guys finally get it and decide to go 'click and mortar,' they'll buy us. Maybe they have money now, but they're not hip to the Internet." He glanced at me to see if he registered any points.

"I'm not sure," I started to say.

"How smart do you have to be," Allison jumped in, "to sell caskets cheap on the Internet? Come on, Lenny."

At first embarrassed, Lenny then glared at her. His entire face glowed red.

She looked at me again and made some sort of decision to go ahead. "Selling cheap caskets isn't what we started out to do," she confessed.

"Wait a minute. We'll get to all that later," Lenny cut in sharply. "Once we land the money and Funerals.com is up and running, then we can evolve the business to content and community. One step at a time. We've talked about this."

"What if we never get to it, Lenny?" she asked. "Things change. Priorities change. The market changes. We'll have our hands full just delivering the e-tailing business. Now is our opportunity."

This turn of discussion clearly made Lenny uncomfortable, but he did nothing to stop it. He knew he needed Allison.

"Let the funeral homes dispose of the remains," Allison continued. "The Internet's never going to take care of that. Let us focus on the emotional needs of the people left behind. That was our starting point for this entire idea, and that's still what we should focus on."

In their early brainstorming, Lenny had convinced Allison that the Internet provided an opportunity for them to address those emotional needs, especially for survivors and friends spread around the world. Many of those people, Allison claimed, want a way to communicate with each other, to remember their loved ones, to come to terms with and sort through the meaning of the death. There were ways to do that on the Internet. Just because family and friends live apart, doesn't mean they have to grieve alone. The core of the business that excited Allison was community, and into the community areas of the site they could build content—information about funerals, about the process and arrangements, the law and regulations, information that would demystify all of it as well as arm consumers.

"Right," Lenny said sarcastically when Allison was done. "And how exactly do you make money with that?"

"If we provide information about counseling services, referrals, places you can go to talk about grief," she added, "that's real value." She hesitated. "Maybe there's a way for family members to share their memories on-line, and some way for people even to address the person who's gone. If we make the site useful, people will return and rely on it, and advertising and commerce opportunities will follow those people."

"On-line séances," Lenny commented, looking at me. "What a great idea."

"Lenny." She was impatient. "Say what you want now. But we talked about all of this, and I thought we agreed."

"I just don't think it's a business," Lenny said.

"And I am not interested in selling cheap caskets and liners," she retorted.

That got Lenny's attention. I suddenly realized he had assumed, despite Allison's reservations, that she would come along if they could raise the money, that she would suspend her hopes indefinitely while they nibbled at a morsel of the original idea.

"I don't think, if we pursued all those ideas we talked about," he said almost belligerently, "we would have gotten even this far."

She was talking about some sort of social agency, he claimed, some not-for-profit meant solely to help people, not make money. They couldn't get funding for that. Who would put up money for that? he demanded to know. She had no ready answer.

"For all the problems with Funerals.com," he went on, "they didn't laugh at us, and we would have been laughed out the door today if we'd come in saying we were going to help people, we were going to fill needs that churches used to fill. How are people going to pay for that? What's the economic model for that?"

He waited for an answer.

"What's it cost to run a site like that?" he went on when she clearly had no answer. "What's the content cost, the infrastructure? How do you find customers? What's your relationship with funeral directors and funeral homes?"

I smiled inwardly because his litany of questions probably echoed the very questions Phil had shot at him that morning.

Allison simply listened to all this with jaw set, shaking her head in incredulity. Obviously she knew Lenny well enough to let him run down a bit before jumping back in.

"Al, I'm not saying we will never do what you want," he offered finally, in what sounded like a closing. "I think we can do it eventually, but I don't believe we can get funded by promoting a business aimed first and foremost at helping people. We have to focus on products, revenue, growth, profits. Your ideas are too squishy. You see this utopia, this company with no structure and a bunch of eager beavers who work for the love of it. What you want is unrealistic. If we win on the bottom line, then we can consider new ideas and directions. Hey, if we're a big success we can even endow a foundation to deal with the virtuous, people aspect of death and dying."

"Lenny, I'm not going to wait a lifetime to bequeath some foundation," she said. They had known each other a long time and didn't pull punches. That could be a good trait among cofounders.

"Besides," Allison continued, "I'm not interested in *funding* a service. I want to spend my time being involved. I want to work in an organization that cares about people in trouble, that"—she waved her arm—"that cares about people, period. This is a chance to change what we don't like." She paused for a moment. "And you're right. I want to build a legacy company, a place we can be proud of, where people work hard, and care about what they do and respect each other. I want a place I can believe in, in every way—what it does, what it stands for, how it works. I don't want to wait for my ship to come in before I can afford to start. Why wait when we can do it now?"

Clearly Lenny had failed to sell her one of his Deferred Life Plans.

They were an even odder combination than I had imagined: Lenny with his one-dimensional, bottom-line view of business, and Allison with her lofty ideals about people.

Lenny glanced at me—clearly fishing for support. Now, as Allison finished her rejoinder, he simply turned to me, shrugged, and held his hands out, palms up, as if to say, "Hopeless. What can I do?"

"I don't think I can help you with this one, Lenny," I said. Maybe ten years ago. Not now.

It was another instance in which, were I still Lenny's age, I would have agreed with him. Sure, business was about money. That's what makes it business. But first and foremost, to be successful, business is about people. It took me a while to learn that lesson.

I STARTED MY BUSINESS career as a negotiator, a deal guy. I was trained to take advantage, to get the upper hand, to beat down the other side. I was an assassin. My job was to win at any cost, and I took some satisfaction in doing it well. I didn't understand much about the human side of business. In my mind, there was not much room for humanity on the bottom line. That point of view didn't particularly comfort me, but that's the way business worked, I thought. Given those constraints, I also figured my days in the world of business were numbered. But before I decided to chuck it all and become some freelance tour guide, I met Bill Campbell.

I was working at Apple, but was on the verge of leaving the legal department because it was restructuring. My boss encouraged me to meet Bill, who, at the time, was leading a spinout of Apple's software applications business. The purpose of the spinout was to reduce Apple's dependence on Microsoft software.

Bill was moving like a lightning bolt to arrange things. He corralled me into an empty conference room, didn't bother to turn on the lights, gave me the three-minute pitch, said I'd come well recommended, and asked whether I'd join him. Now. Given no time to think, I checked my gut and heard myself say, "Yes." Without any details about the job, my title, or my compensation. As Bill marched off, I heard him say, "Great. You're the first cofounder. Let's get moving." It turned out to be one of my best decisions ever.

We called the company Claris, and we had big dreams. We were going to beat Microsoft by employing the philosophy of the Apple computer and operating system: making the power of the technology accessible by creating great software that was easy to use, not just stuffed with complicated arcane features few people wanted or needed. A key part of my job at Claris, of course, involved doing deals. I negotiated the spinout agreement with Apple, and I negotiated Claris's acquisitions of technology and of numerous software companies, both of which were key strategies for building the business.

I barely knew Campbell, but others called him "Coach," ostensibly because he had been the head coach of Columbia's football team, but in reality because of his dedication to mentoring his people. He was in his mid-forties, stern to eye, but warm and caring through and through. He wore his countless football scars and rugby wounds like badges of honor. You'd follow this guy anywhere.

And we did. What you noticed about Bill, after you worked with him a bit, was that he spent a lot of time talking about people. He ate, drank, and breathed people. You couldn't talk about anything at Claris without the issue coming up. I found it irritating at first, a distraction. Whenever we sat down to make decisions, somebody always asked, How is this going to affect that individual, or this group of people? What are they going to say? To feel? Will they know why you made that decision or will they think you did it arbitrarily? When we talked about product support, it wasn't evaluated as an expense line. It was a service—for people. The focus was always on the value you could deliver to your customers, employees, partners, and shareholders—and what they and others thought about it and about you. You might not hear it in the first session. You might not hear it in the second session. But, unless you were deaf, by the end of the first few months, you heard the theme loud and clear. Bill had an underlying faith that if we focused on the people issues, worked hard, and did a great job, the business would take care of itself. That was Campbell.

In the beginning, despite my respect for him, I resisted Bill's philosophy. I strongly believed in the notion of business as a manageable, predictable, and quantifiable process. I believed everything should be crisp, clear, and buttoned down. Managers made the trains run on time. Campbell's approach seemed inefficient to me. Too many soft, murky, and complicated issues to grapple with. Let's just focus on the stuff we can measure, I contended.

For some reason, Campbell, thank goodness, didn't give up on me. There were times he probably should have fired me because I was such a pain in the ass. My work brought me in contact with all parts of Claris, and I would outspokenly and constantly challenge anything that didn't appear to contribute directly to the bottom line. I was often out of step with Bill and the rest of the executive team.

But I gradually began to internalize Campbell's frame of mind, and some of my own personal values, long subordinated to the bottom line, began to resurface. I couldn't argue with Bill's results: What appeared to be a sometimes inefficient process was creating extraordinary success. Our customers liked us. They valued our products. Our partners respected and trusted us.

Our employees were highly motivated and committed. Often I would be working late, and I'd look up from my computer at eleven or twelve at night to see a crowd, all working just as feverishly. Why was I there late? Because I needed to finish my piece of a project, so I could hand it over to somebody else, so she could get on with what she needed to do, so the next person could do what he needed to do, so the company could achieve its objectives. There was an intense sense of loyalty, responsibility, and camaraderie; a locking of elbows with everybody around you.

The change in my perception of Campbell is summed up by one of my favorite Mark Twain quotes: "When I was a boy of fourteen, my father was so ignorant I could hardly stand to have the old man around. But when I got to be twenty-one, I was astonished at how much he had learned in seven years." Likewise, in a short time I had learned what wisdom Campbell carried; he could do things I couldn't quantify. He had a highly intuitive sense of people. He could inspire them to be better than they already were and to work together as a whole to create something greater than the sum of the individual parts.

Still, some lessons came hard. We had an opportunity to buy a company called Quark, a pioneer in the then-new software category of desktop publishing. I stayed up all night and flew to Denver to get a letter of intent signed. It would be a great deal. But subsequently, when we entered into definitive negotiations, we stumbled on the issue of warranties. They wouldn't give me something I believed they should. I was indignant. I remember telling them, "I'm paying you good money, you're selling me the company, and you've got to agree that what you're selling me is yours to give." They were offended. They thought they were joining the Claris team; that's what they said they wanted to do. But my focus on the warranty issues—on the cold, hard facts of business, on getting the best deal—estranged them and made them feel like outsiders. We went back and forth a bit, and then they simply refused to work with me anymore. Bill stepped in to try to save the deal, but it couldn't be saved. I had blown it irretrievably. The disagreement could have been mitigated with other legal remedies, but I had adamantly opposed them on principle, and there was no backtracking. That was a dumb mistake. Quark would have been an incredible asset for Claris.

In addition to a sense of professional failure—this was the first time I had ever blown a deal—I felt I had let down *my* company. I had let *us* down. It was *our* deal, and I dropped the ball for everybody, including myself, in the process.

I started to pay attention. I made a break with my old legal habits. I began to apply Campbell's thinking to doing deals. My job was to find intersections of interest between the negotiating parties—not differences, but commonalities—and to build them into a solid relationship and transaction. I started zeroing in immediately on those requirements of the other party that were consistent with my requirements, and I threw my energy into bringing them into the deal, instead of ignoring them or reactively opposing them in order to use them as bargaining chips later. My focus became less on just satisfying myself and my company and more on satisfying the other party as well. Sure, certain points were bound to be contentious, but negotiating became a creative opportunity for me to solve problems and build relationships, not to play poker.

My final Claris lesson came when we sold the company back to Apple. We had intended initially that Claris would eventually go public. But when Apple discovered in our draft prospectus that we planned to develop software for Windows, not just for the Macintosh, Apple execs decided to reel us back in rather than suffer the embarrassment of watching their offspring consort with the enemy. They had the contractual right to do so; however, the spinout agreement we had negotiated forced them to pay a multiple of the anticipated IPO price for the privilege. It was a lucrative deal for all of us.

But it was a Pyrrhic victory. With our spouses, we all gathered at the home of one of the founders to celebrate our good fortune. Together we drank the celebration into a wake. We were proud of the price we'd gotten from Apple—there was reason to celebrate—but when we looked around the room at each other, the deal's downside hit us: it was unlikely we would ever work together again. The exhilarating experience of the Claris startup made few of us eager to return to the larger Apple fold.

Our checks were in the bank, but we were morose. What the heck was that, I wondered?

Campbell had a better bead than any of us on what was happening. He knew he'd given up his baby, even as the rest of us were skirting around the edges of that loss. I later realized what a rare privilege it had been to work with this group of people, in a place of our own making that gave us the opportunity to reach and stretch, to have impact, and to be great. Building a $90-million-a-year, market-leading business was a hard thing to do. Claris gave us, as a team and as individuals, a platform for growing and a chance to build a legacy and a culture that would contain our DNA in its values for decades to come. You couldn't put a price on it, and I didn't realize that until our company was dead and buried.

BUSINESS, I told Lenny and Allison, is about nothing if not people. First, the people you serve, your market. Then the team you build, your employees. Finally, your many business partners and associates. Sever the chain of values between leadership and the people translating strategy into products and services for your customers, and you will destroy your foundation for long-term success. The culture you create and principles you express are the only connection you will have with each other and your many constituencies. It may not be Allison's utopia, but it was a far cry from Lenny's soulless machine.

As I talked, Lenny had been sneaking looks at his watch. "We'll have to continue this discussion another time," Lenny said. They needed to be off to the airport for the flight home, to arrive in Boston at midnight. Coast-to-coast day-tripping was a hard life.

He and Allison stood and thanked me for my time and help.

"Lot to think about," Lenny changed the subject. "I'm very optimistic. I believe this is going to happen. I can feel it."

I wasn't sure he had heard a word I said.

Connie drifted by as they were walking away.

"Got the money, huh?" she said.

Clambering into his rental Neon, Lenny gave us a big grin and a thumbs-up.

I could only shake my head.

Chapter Eight

The Art
of
Leadership

I SPENT THE REST of the afternoon in a long, drawn out session with Chris, the founder of one of the companies I work with. He had enough problems and challenges to push any thoughts of Lenny temporarily from my mind.

Chris had done a terrific job building a core team, raising seed capital, developing patented technology, and launching an Internet service for the on-line searching of audio/video content. But the business wasn't happening, and he was not up to the task of bringing in strategic industry partners—big portals and entertainment sites. Sales were negligible. Chris was an engineer with a great concept, but he was running out of steam. His management team was having second thoughts, given the lack of progress in the market.

The company needed new leadership, badly. While Chris was able intellectually to concede this, it was hard for him emotionally to deliver his baby to someone else's charge. As much as the company needed a new CEO, it couldn't afford to lose Chris's creative vision and passion. I couldn't separate Chris's success from the company's success. We had come to that quintessential tough moment in a startup's maturation you hope won't occur: time for the founder to consider giving up the reins.

Silicon Valley veterans share a tacit understanding that what a startup needs isn't one CEO, but three—each at successive stages of the startup's development. Given my deep regard for man's best friend, I tend to think of each in terms of best of breed. The first CEO is "the Retriever." From the muck she must assemble the core team, the product or service, and the market direction—all around a coherent vision. She must also raise the money and secure crucial early customers and partners. She is prized for her tenacity and inventiveness. The second CEO is "the Bloodhound." He must *sniff out* a trail—find the market and prove the business. He needs to build an operating team and establish a market beachhead. He is prized for his keen sense of direction and company-building skills. The third CEO is "the Husky." She must lead the team, pulling an operating company that grows heavier by the day with people and public company responsibilities. She is prized for her constancy and scalability. None of these, to me, is top dog. All are equal in importance, just different in skills and temperaments. I mentor the founding CEO so she can go as far as she wants or as far as her abilities permit. And when she decides to pass the mantle, I help with the transition to new leadership. We all hope, when that time comes, the company won't need a Saint Bernard.

After hours of discussion with Chris, there still wasn't any resolution. I didn't arrive home until nearly dinnertime, and I was mentally exhausted. I piled my stuff on the dining room table, patted the hounds, poured a glass of Merlot, and sank into my office chair. On autopilot, I hit the power button and logged on. My inbox held a message from Frank.

TO: randy@virtual.net
FROM: frank@vcfirm.com
SUBJECT: Deceased

Randy,

FYI, Lenny pitched the partners this morning. We'd like to do something with this market, but I think we're going to pass on Funerals.com. Lenny's probably got some potential, a diamond in the rough. Maybe too rough. He still doesn't seem to have a good way of coming to grips with this opportunity. Not sure he knows where to go with it. And if he doesn't know, we just can't get excited. Thanks for your help.

I have another deal I'd like you to look at. Gimme a call.

Frank

I wished Lenny were here now, so I could grab him by the lapels and tell him to pay attention.

Lenny was right in assuming that Frank and the other VCs

weren't running charitable institutions. But the best learned through trial and error that investing in a passionate group of smart people, with a big idea for a big market, provided the greatest odds for success. Lenny was shortchanging himself and Allison by focusing on how to build an opportunistic business, a casket discounter. Sure it might work, but Frank and his partners had bigger fish to fry. Lenny needed to embrace his earlier, bigger idea. At least there was something in that to sink your teeth into, something worth working hard for.

To: frank@vcfirm.com
From: randy@virtual.net
SUBJECT: A Second Life

Frank,

I understand completely and agree.

Still, a second discussion with Lenny--along with Allison--makes me suspect that Lenny may be his own worst enemy.

What if their business were about building communities for families and friends coping with the deaths of loved ones? A content site and directory of local services? What if it gave families a place to gather from wherever they were, anywhere in the world, where they could share their grief and help each other make arrangements and decisions? This could include family Web pages and chat. What if the revenues came not only from the commerce they're talking about now, but also from the advertising of support

```
services, providing qualified leads to
people who can help, and delivering
premium on-line services to interested
parties? I don't know what those are
yet, but if the site got up and run-
ning, the users would tell us. This
business could work in partnership with
local providers of related services and
funeral directors, and lock them all
into a referral network.

Just curious.

best

r
```

I had no idea how Frank would respond, but if he passed on this deal, I wanted to make sure he was rejecting the big idea lurking beneath the surface of Funerals.com, and not Lenny's superficial version of it.

Both Debra and I were home for dinner for once. As she sorted through the mail, I rallied every pan in the house. With a bottle of Napa Valley sauvignon blanc, we ate outside as the sun set without a fuss.

Later that evening, still digesting, I sank into my leather chair with a book by the thirteenth-century Zen master Dogen, my quiet house open to the light breeze stealing in off the hills. The low timpani of snoring dogs signaled that the world was just fine.

Dogen's brain-numbing insights eluded me. I couldn't get past his notion of time: "Do not think that time merely flies away. Do not see flying away as the only function of time. If time merely flies away, you would be separated from time."

Another monk's riddle—I needed something a lot less chal-
lenging tonight.

There is always e-mail.

I trod lightly so as not to disturb the hounds. But who was
I kidding? They were dead to the world, expecting me to take
the first watch. The old PowerBook took a few extra minutes
to fire up. My Mac was not long for this world.

Just a few messages, including a response from Frank, had
dropped in since I had last checked a couple of hours earlier.

TO: randy@virtual.net
FROM: frank@vcfirm.com
SUBJECT: Re: A Second Life

Randy,

Interesting. The content and community
aspects are appealing--playing to the
Internet's strengths. Incorporating the
local services also sounds good. I can
definitely see some network effect
here. Makes a win-win and a more defensible referral channel. Obviously has
to be fleshed out, but more intriguing.

Unfortunately, it's not the
Funerals.com Lenny presented. Is it
yours or Lenny's? Lenny seems stuck on
the casket business. Who will lead
this?

Frank

Who will lead this?

Good question. I knew Lenny's answer based on the org

chart in his plan, but Lenny had not yet demonstrated that he had the right stuff. He was trying to reduce the challenge of starting Funerals.com to rote execution, and he was focusing on managing the process. But this was a startup. It would take an inspirational leader to rally a team and supporters to build something worthwhile. So far, Lenny had failed to inspire any of us.

Management and leadership are related but not identical. Lenny's vantage point from the bowels of the Borg, though, had never given him an appreciation for the difference. Management is a methodical process; its purpose is to produce the desired results on time and on budget. It complements and supports but cannot do without leadership, in which character and vision combine to empower someone to venture into uncertainty. Leaders must suspend the disbelief of their constituents and move ahead even with very incomplete information.

From the start, Lenny had set out to manage Funerals.com; he assumed that management ability was what Frank and I wanted most to see in him. He aggressively pared back the early vision that had brought Allison and him to the business in the first place, in order to make it more manageable. His business had become so focused that when he couldn't anticipate how something would be managed, he excluded it from the plan and the business altogether. The result? Funerals.com was a laser beam pointed at a very narrow, easily defined e-tailer idea. And it failed to excite Allison, or me, or Frank and his partners. Truth be told, it didn't excite Lenny either, except for the prospect of that pot of gold.

Like Lenny, I had, early in my career, failed to appreciate the crucial distinction between leadership and management. Luckily I had the good fortune to work with Bill Campbell long enough to learn the difference.

After Apple reabsorbed Claris, Bill became the CEO of GO Corporation, the pioneer in what was hailed as the next megabillion dollar industry, pen computing. Bill asked me to join him as CFO and VP of Business Operations. As Bill's inside guy, I kept everything tuned: creating the plan, raising the money, doing the deals, and running the numbers. In short, I executed.

GO was formed to create a new and more intuitive way for people to operate computers, using a pen for input and navigation instead of a keyboard and a mouse. GO's vision spawned a mad rush to this seductive new interface. Before long AT&T, IBM, Microsoft, Apple, and many others had joined the fray. In the two years I was there, GO grew significantly, burning more than $2 million a month. Before it was over, we had raised over $75 million—a phenomenal sum for that time. The vision was brilliant, but the technology for handwriting recognition wasn't up to the task. We were dancing as fast as we could, but it became clear to many of us that GO was unlikely to succeed. Yet Bill's leadership was so powerful that no one from the management team bailed out. This was a group of talented people, most of whom went on to leadership roles at other companies, including their own successful startups. But because of Bill, no one pulled the cord. Everyone rode that plane all the way down to a belly landing.

When I finally did leave GO in 1993, it wasn't clear what I wanted to do next. In the years we worked together, Campbell had periodically suggested that I consider becoming a CEO. He had encouraged me to prepare for the role by giving me projects and responsibilities that would help me run a business at some point. Perhaps misery loves company, but for Bill, being a CEO was one of the most fun and satisfying roles he'd ever played. I was flattered by his suggestion, but I was hardly your prototypical M.B.A. with an unquenchable drive to prove myself as a captain of industry.

I wanted a role full of creativity, where inspiration was more valued than perspiration. I was intrigued by the digital "content" business, the emerging idea that computers could deliver useful information and engaging entertainment, not just applications. Sniffing around, I realized that digital content would be the next big door to open in the marketplace. I bought some PC games and CD-ROMs, which were just becoming popular as founts of rich content, and discovered some fascinating experiments in interactivity. Games were the first incarnation of this new medium, but I saw an opportunity to create many other strains of interactive, digital content.

Out of the blue, a headhunter called looking for a CEO for a game company called LucasArts Entertainment, located in Marin county, just north of San Francisco. This was the electronic games division of George Lucas's entertainment business. The headhunter was desperate because LucasArts had rejected all his usual suspects. I was his long shot. I couldn't understand why the company would have any interest in me, but he persisted. So, in one of my only remaining suits from my lawyer days, now ill-fitting and out of fashion, I met with the LucasArts hiring committee. As its members described the company, the mystery of their interest in me only deepened. The job description unequivocally excluded me. I didn't have the experience they wanted, and I wasn't a gamer. Still, they asked to meet again. The headhunter suggested I lose the suit.

Concerned about the apparent mismatch between the position and me, I discussed the pros and cons with a close friend from GO, Debbie Biondolillo. A wonderful woman with a wealth of common sense, she had been in charge of

HR at GO, and before that was an HR vice president at Apple. I gave her the spiel I intended to deliver to the hiring committee. It focused on the underpinnings of the LucasArts business model, product strategy, and distribution arrangements.

"That's all very insightful. Solid thinking," Debbie commented when I finished. "But they're looking for the CEO. They're looking for the leader. What's your vision? What's the big idea? How will you get people excited? They'll want to hear where you intend to take them as a company."

I was a wise, old hand when it came to solving tactical issues. That had always been my job as a manager. Now I was being asked to lead and motivate, to create a vision that could attract and inspire talent and partners. Managing—vigorously driving execution—is a rare skill, Debbie told me, but rarer still is the ability to lead, inspire, and motivate people.

So I sat down with a blank piece of paper and started working out my ideas. I concocted a diagram about the evolution of interactive storytelling—concentric circles showing how interactive storytelling was or could be different from other forms of storytelling and other media. It was a crude chart, but it seemed to make sense. It excited me, both because of what it said and because I'd forgotten how much I enjoyed that free-form way of thinking.

After some soul searching—developing a vision that excited me was certainly a factor—I decided to proceed with the interview process, which meant meeting the myth himself. I rode my motorcycle to Skywalker Ranch, buzzing with ideas for LucasArts. I had a plan to expand on the creative strengths of the organization and to drive the medium in a way consistent with George Lucas's storytelling legacy. With LucasArts we would accomplish for the video game business what Industrial Light & Magic had done for the movie special-effects business. The Lucas brand would become a haven for a new breed of creative talent excelling in interactive storytelling.

When I finally met with George, I couldn't stop talking. I whipped out my charts. I ran on about interactive storytelling and my vision for the medium. George, who had of course already given the topic a lot of thought, engaged with me in a lively give-and-take about the future of games and interactive content. Whether it was my vision and enthusiasm or simply LucasArts' desperation, I don't know, but I was eventually offered the helm.

No CEO's job is all vision, though, and my job at LucasArts included considerable management efforts. We almost immediately restructured our domestic distribution strategy and renegotiated our international distribution deals, improving our margins and control significantly and thereby putting us in a better position to attract outside products for redistribution under the Lucas label. We engaged our own sales force. These moves were controversial, given that Lucas had never invested in anything other than the creative side of the business, but they turned out to be a stroke of good timing when our earlier distributor went under just as we were releasing our summer hit product, TIE Fighter.

Next we greenlighted a sequel to the company's CD-ROM megahit, Rebel Assault, against the protests of many in the company. Once again, we were fortunate, and the sequel turned out to be a huge seller. We set up a new group to develop an edutainment CD, a first for the company. We hired a "Next Generation" development team and struck a deal with Nintendo to be a preferred developer and partner in a Star Wars title for their impending juggernaut game console, the Ultra 64.

I struggled to build consensus at every step, but I knew that ultimately I had to earn everyone's confidence through results. With hard work and good luck, the results came. In less than two years we catapulted the company to the number one PC game publisher and increased sales and earnings by a factor of three or four.

I liked being the leader better than being the guy who made the trains run on time. I found that the art wasn't in getting the numbers to foot, or figuring out a clever way to move something down the assembly line. It was in getting somebody else to do that and to do it better than I could ever do; in encouraging people to exceed their own expectations; in inspiring people to be great; and in getting them to do it all together, in harmony. That was the high art.

Lenny would need to step up and make a similar transformation. He would have to take on the mantle of leader and rally people to his vision to enlist their support. He could not hope to get by simply trying to make the train run; he would have to set its course and motivate others to join him for the ride. It would be easy to dismiss him as no Jack Welch, but if he could become the Retriever and assemble Funerals.com from the muck, he would be the right CEO for phase one. The time to worry about operating leadership would come in the company's next phase.

WORKING WITH Steve Perlman at WebTV taught me how critical it is in an early-stage startup to strike the right balance between leadership and management.

I met Steve at Apple in 1986 when he was a young whiz kid, one of the more inspired inventors, in the Advanced Development Group. We stayed in touch over the years. In the spring of 1995, just after I started at Crystal Dynamics, Steve invited me to his house for a peek at his latest top-secret project. In his study, crammed with wires, electronic boards, and gadgets from Fry's Computer Store, he showed me the Playboy Web site.

Checking out the Playboy site was commonplace among early Web surfers, but Steve was doing it with one critical improvement: there it was in his study on a television set. In creatively marrying two disparate technologies never designed to work together, the computer and the television, Steve had just made the Internet available to every couch potato. Suddenly it was possible for the Net to touch anyone with a TV set, not just those with computers and the savvy to use them.

Steve and his partners were founding Artemis Research, ultimately WebTV, to pursue his invention. Lacking experience in operating a business, he wanted me to join as CEO. As excited as I was about his vision for the Internet on television, and as fond as I was of him, I had to beg off because I had just taken the CEO gig at Crystal Dynamics. I did, however, advise him and his team on building the company, and shortly afterward I joined the WebTV board. Steve called me often to seek advice about specific operational issues—financing, business plans, negotiations, hiring. He proved a quick study.

A year later, as I left Crystal, Steve asked me again to join as CEO. Not an easy decision this time. He was a natural, inspirational leader, and his charismatic vision attracted the best talent, investors, and supporters. But given his role as company visionary, my job, if I had become CEO, would have been primarily operational, more like my role at GO than at LucasArts. I had to decline.

Still, WebTV was growing rapidly, hiring a couple of hundred people and raising over $100 million dollars in the first couple of years, and Steve needed someone who had lived through it before. So, without taking a formal position, I increased my involvement to help with operating issues, and that's when Steve gave me the "Virtual CEO" business cards.

This was a quintessential "Brave New World" company. Despite its rapid growth, WebTV's business model was still largely undefined. No one knew how it would finally make money. The hardware was far costlier to make than our wholesale price to distributors. Profits would have to come from services provided through the box, but which services and at what price were still unclear.

In this uncertainty, Steve shined. To call him a technical leader did not do him justice. Technology was not the sole source of his success. He was in fact a brilliant promoter—part Edison, part P. T. Barnum. He could inspire investors and employees based on a mesmerizing vision that, for the moment, made everyone forget the absence of a clear economic model. In round after round of financing, Steve was always able to sell a higher valuation than I thought possible and bring in critical partners.

Supporting Steve, I felt a strong obligation to investors and employees to rationalize the business quickly. We needed to make economic sense of it, and better sooner than later. Steve resisted. He insisted on evolving his vision for the Internet on television and exploring its potential before constraining himself and the company with a bottom-line operating mentality.

One day, in the middle of my wrestling with building a business around Internet TV, Steve walked in and announced, "It's not the Net on TV, it's Enhanced TV."

What the heck is Enhanced Television?

His new, broader vision included but went far beyond the Net on TV. At its core was the notion that information could flow back and forth between the service or program source and the viewer. No longer wholly passive, the viewer would be able to interact with the television. Interactive programming would be served up from the Internet and seamlessly connect with video programming from cable, satellite, and terrestrial broadcast. Viewers could chat with their favorite soap stars, get behind-the-scenes glimpses of celebrities, explore the historical background for the events in a movie, or peruse a mountain of statistics while watching a game.

At first I dismissed Enhanced TV as Steve's folly, yet another frustrating distraction from our attempts to make WebTV into a real, operating enterprise. Of course, Steve persisted, and, finally, I realized he was right. The Net on TV had the disadvantage of introducing a new service to the living room, where it would need time to gain a foothold. The ultimate market was probably small; not that many couch potatoes were dying to surf the Net. But enhanced television offered to take a ubiquitous, well-understood medium—television—and make it better. Enhanced Television was about 100 million households. A big idea.

The problem was that while increasing our market opportunity Steve had also increased the complexity of the business by an order of magnitude. How would you connect television programming with the Internet in a compelling way? Where would the content come from? How would you cover the costs of additional storage in the set-top box needed to accommodate it all? My head spinning, I could see a river of red ink gushing down the halls like blood in *The Shining*. We would need a billion dollars, not $100 to $200 million. I didn't know how to raise a billion dollars.

Microsoft, it turns out, had been thinking along similar lines, though its view was largely focused on the computer as an alternative to the television set—a view Steve thought was silly. As WebTV began evangelizing Enhanced Television, with its ability to combine Internet content and television programming, Microsoft, realizing it could have the best of both worlds, approached Steve about buying his company. Steve was reluctant to give up control but finally, after a great deal of agonizing, he decided to sell. In the end he knew making Enhanced TV successful was going to cost a fortune, if it worked at all. Microsoft's deep pockets would give him a shot at it. We weren't sure we could ever pay the tab otherwise.

If Steve had ceded his visionary leadership to an operating manager early on, Microsoft probably would never have bought WebTV. Limiting ourselves to the Internet television business would have shortchanged Steve's larger vision, and WebTV would have had to struggle with building a much smaller and just as risky business on its own.

For me, the moral of the story of Steve Perlman and WebTV is the need to emphasize visionary leadership over management acumen in the formative stage of a startup. If you turn a visionary startup into an operating company too early, you throw out its birthright. It will never be as big, as grand, or as influential as it might otherwise be. It will be much harder, perhaps impossible, to expand the vision later, when performance is being measured quarter to quarter against operating plans, because then there's too much at stake. Steve was the right leader, the only leader, to take WebTV through its formative years.

LENNY, of course, was leaning entirely in the opposite direction. He'd taken a big idea and shrunk it to make operational sense of it before he even started. In the process, he'd gutted his big idea and reduced his potential. He had yet to demonstrate his ability to develop a compelling vision worth following. Could he lead?

In my last check of the night, I found an e-mail from him. I was betting he had heard from Frank, though I suspected Frank's message was less direct than his "we're going to pass" message to me. Lenny probably had gotten the hedge-your-bets "no."

TO: randy@virtual.net
FROM: lenny@alchemy.net
SUBJECT: Dead Wrong

Randy,

Got home tonight and found a note from Frank. I'm confused. He says I should feel free to "explore other possibili-ties." When do we get the money?

Thanks,

Lenny

I hit "Reply" and tapped out a response.

TO: lenny@alchemy.net
FROM: randy@virtual.net
SUBJECT: Re: Dead Wrong

I cannot speak for Frank. But my assessment is that nothing is going to happen there for you, Lenny. Frank's telling you nicely to go somewhere else. My sense is that, in your two attempts, you've failed to excite any-one with Funerals.com.

Sorry for the bluntness, and I may be wrong, but I doubt it.

My advice: Go back to why you and
Allison started on this path in the
first place, to the things she was
talking about at the Konditorei, and
try to recapture some of that. Valuable
content and a vibrant community can
establish a strong following that you
can monetize with commerce and advertising. Where there's a critical mass,
there's money.

Stop playing it safe. Don't waste your
time or Frank's.

Ask yourself the question: What would
make you willing to do Funerals.com for
the rest of your life? Start from
there.

best

r
_____

Chapter Nine

THE GAMBLE

WHEN MY MIND finally turned to business the next morning, my first thoughts were of Lenny. I knew he was at a crossroads. I had no affinity for Funerals.com, at least as Lenny had cast it, but Allison had struck a chord with me. Her enthusiasm for a community-based service was real; so was her disappointment in the evisceration of their original dream. If Lenny truly shared Allison's vision, I wanted very much for them to get a shot at it. On the other hand, if Lenny couldn't get past his limited view, better to part ways now and put Funerals.com to rest. Lenny was going to have to answer those fundamental questions he had so neatly avoided thus far. Why was he doing this? What was important to him, and what did he care about? Who was he, and how could he express that in his business? I was now curious about the answers.

But when I checked my inbox, there was nothing from Lenny. To my surprise, though, there was a message from Allison. I opened it immediately.

TO: randy@virtual.net
FROM: awhitlock@digger.net
SUBJECT: One Last Question

Randy,

Thanks for meeting with us the other day. I hope you understand my position. In his frenzy to get Funerals.com funded and operating, Lenny won't consider anything not directly on point. To be honest, I find it demoralizing.

Lenny forwarded your e-mail regarding the outcome of the VC meeting. I'm sorry for Lenny, but I wasn't surprised.

Unfortunately, Lenny now seems paralyzed with indecision. He finally hit a wall he can't break through, and it's shaken him up. As much as I know he'll deny it, I think he needs someone else to call this one.

What do you think I should do? I'd like to take your advice and give the community concept a run. There's nothing else for me in this anyway, and if we can get support for the business that

This was a promising turn of events. Allison's job offer was in the bag, and yet she was still willing to gamble on their original business vision. I wondered if Lenny was equally willing to take the risk. In the Deferred Life Plan, by definition, you postpone risking what matters most to you; that happens later, if it happens at all. What if Lenny pursued a business built around what truly mattered to him, and it failed? What if the world told him, despite his absolute best efforts, that what most inspired his passion wasn't very interesting? With Funerals.com, Lenny had been minimizing his exposure and avoiding the real test. He was aiming far too low.

My morning was unscheduled, so I decided to escape from e-mail for a while. I suited up and grabbed my racing bike for a brisk ride in the hills. I do some of my best thinking while pedaling.

The first leg of my route was up Page Mill Road, a winding climb to over two thousand feet, through oak forests, with an occasional glimpse of the Bay shimmering in the morning sun. Cycling has long been my favorite way to travel, and I had logged thousands of miles zigzagging throughout New England, Eastern Canada, and even China during the seventies and early eighties. I put my love of travel on hold, though, while I pursued my Valley career. A few years ago, I reshuffled the cards when I became a Virtual CEO and recalibrated my priorities and passions. Since then I have biked France, Spain, Vietnam, Laos, and Myanmar. Soon, Bhutan, and who knows where else?

As my legs spun, my mind churned on the idea of risk. Everything in this Valley turns on risk. Lenny had been hedging, unwilling to expose the big idea, because he suspected it had a substantial chance of failing as a business. Cheaper caskets seemed straightforward as a moneymaker, and he wouldn't have to stretch hard to try it. Proposing a business with higher aspirations seemed too risky because it wasn't clear how that business, the one he and Allison first discussed, the one that had excited them, could work. So Lenny focused on the bottom line in an attempt to appeal to what he presumed to be Frank's greed. He underestimated Frank and the importance of vision, passion, and the big idea. The question he seemed to have answered was not, How can I make a difference? but, What's the least risky path to financial success? Ironically, he had assumed the biggest risk of all in Silicon Valley, the risk of mediocrity. He had dug his own grave.

Lenny didn't understand how the Valley thinks about business risk and failure. Instead of managing business risk to minimize or avoid failure, the focus here is on maximizing success. The Valley recognizes that failure is an unavoidable part of the search for success.

Silicon Valley does not punish business failure. It punishes stupidity, laziness, and dishonesty. Failure is inevitable if you are trying to invent the future. The Valley forgives business failures that arise from natural causes and acts of God: changes, for example, in the market, competition, or technology. The key question here is *why* a business failed. When you have a big idea as GO had, and you turn out to be years ahead of the market, failure doesn't end careers. Ironically, businesses that fail for acceptable reasons can actually provide a wealth of experience and increased opportunities, as was the case for all the key players at GO.

Ted Williams once said baseball was the only human endeavor at which one could fail 70 percent of the time and still be a success. To baseball I would add the venture capital business, in which only two or three in ten of all funded business ideas eventually hit big, the Internet phenomenon notwithstanding. For the investor, the explanation of this paradox is simple: the lonely winners return 10 to 100 times or more what the losers lose. With those odds you can see how the VC business and the Valley work. And if you understand that, you can understand how VCs evaluate business ideas. They want something that will make a difference, and not a small difference. Hedging is not the way to get their attention. Reducing your downside risk will not warm the cockles of their hearts. Business failures are unfortunate but necessary steps in the search for those few huge successes.

I reached the top of Page Mill Road and turned north on Skyline, along the ridge of hills that mark the volatile San Andreas Fault. These hills, the result of the millennia-long collision of tectonic plates, literally define Silicon Valley to the east and shield it from the Pacific Ocean on the west. This ridge is part of a plate drifting inexorably toward Alaska.

For some of us, Silicon Valley's forgiving attitude toward failure rests on a more profound realization: Change is certain, and in a world of constant change we actually control very little. When there are important factors outside your control, the risk of failure always looms, no matter how smart or industrious you are. We delude ourselves if we believe that much of life and its key events fall under our control.

Most people will respond to that statement by saying, "Of course. Obviously." Yet many still believe that those who enjoy exceptional achievements and accomplishments rode to the top entirely by themselves. The media always look for a single person, a CEO or an entrepreneur, to personify the accomplishments of an entire company or industry. It makes good reading, but it's simplistic. Someone in the Valley suddenly finds himself worth $100 million dollars and begins to believe he earned, and therefore deserves, that money because of his skill and ability. The rest of the world, egged on by the media, tends to be seduced by the myth, despite the hard work of many others and the role of simple dumb luck. How many of these people accept equal responsibility for the failures in their lives? When you experience the vagaries of success and failure firsthand, it is as hard to accept credit for success as it is to accept blame for failure.

For a long time, I certainly took full credit for my success. I became a lawyer, an expert in the rules that govern the game, worked at Apple in its heyday, and then helped build a highly successful startup at Claris. All that convinced me that I could determine my own fate. It was at GO that I finally realized there were forces at work far larger than anything I, or anyone else, could control. Riding the highs and lows long enough, never being able to see beyond the next peak or the next valley, makes one realize there is only one element in life under our control—our own excellence.

Here's what I tell the founders in the companies I work with about business risk and success, and what Lenny needs to understand: If you're brilliant, 15 to 20 percent of the risk is removed. If you work twenty-four hours a day, another 15 to 20 percent of the risk is removed. The remaining 60 to 70 percent of business risk will be completely out of your control.

My father's a gambler, I tell them, a blackjack player. The game is always in the house's favor. If you play blackjack consistently, you can only lose. Unless you are, like my father, a card counter. He plays the ebbs and flows of the opportunity based on some probability he continuously calculates in his head as he watches the cards dealt. By playing each hand to the best of his ability, he is ready to take advantage of the odds the instant they swing in his favor, wagering more when luck smiles on him, and building his winnings in those moments. Of course, the casinos have made it harder by increasing the number of decks in the shoe and reducing the number of hands played before reshuffling. Nevertheless, my father plugs away, his love of the game unvanquished, waiting impatiently for his chance to win.

If you're excellent at what you do *and* the stars are in alignment, you will win. Of course, you may run out of time first, but, if you're excellent every day, you will have furthered your chances of beating the house as much as they ever can be. That should be your primary measure of success — excellence — not simply the spoils that come with good fortune. You don't want to entrust your satisfaction and sense of fulfillment to circumstances outside your control. Instead, base them on the quality of what you do and who you are, not the success of your business per se. Unless you understand what is truly outside your control, you are likely to make serious mistakes, misallocate resources, and waste time.

I ENCOURAGE PEOPLE to think about all the risks involved — personal risks as well as business risks. When I talk to candidates as part of recruiting outside management talent to the Valley, the issue of risk often comes up. Prospective managers usually fear that the venture won't be a blockbuster or, worse, that it will be forced to close its doors. Some recruits fixate on that business risk to the point of indecision. They strain to research all the facts, but at some point no additional information or assurances will offer them any further clues into the business's ultimate success or failure. Uncertain, they freeze and stay with the status quo, no matter how unsatisfying it is. After all, it's what they know.

But when I drill down, I inevitably find *personal* risks that need to be considered along with the business risks. Personal risks include the risk of working with people you don't respect; the risk of working for a company whose values are inconsistent with your own; the risk of compromising what's important; the risk of doing something you don't care about; and the risk of doing something that fails to express—or even contradicts—who you are. And then there is the most dangerous risk of all—the risk of spending your life not doing what you want on the bet you can buy yourself the freedom to do it later.

Several years ago when I pondered the offer to join Apple, and I looked down that long corridor at my law firm, the answer was clear. I was not concerned with whether Apple's business would succeed or fail or whether my options would be valuable or not. What I had to weigh was whether I should remain on the well-defined path to professional and financial success as a lawyer or venture into a creative life in business, with no specific destination in mind. I was not hesitating because of business risk; I was wrestling with personal risk, a different game of chance in which we have far more control.

When I considered the risk of staying at my law firm, I had to face the possibility of an unfulfilled life, of working endlessly on things that did not matter and that at times violated my core values. I had to face subordinating my creativity in order to become a specialist, channeling myself too narrowly. To me these were graver risks than whether Apple succeeded or failed. Ultimately I chose to pursue what seemed most important to my life at the time.

In theory, the risk of business failure can be reduced to a number, the probability of failure multiplied by the cost of failure. Sure, this turns out to be a subjective analysis, but in the process your own attitudes toward financial risk and reward are revealed.

By contrast, personal risk usually defies quantification. It's a matter of values and priorities, an expression of who you are. "Playing it safe" may simply mean you do not weigh heavily the compromises inherent in the status quo. The financial rewards of the moment may fully compensate you for the loss of time and fulfillment. Or maybe you just don't think about it. On the other hand, if time and satisfaction are precious, truly priceless, you will find that the cost of business failure, so long as it does not put in peril the well-being of you or your family, pales in comparison with the personal risks of not trying to live the life you want today.

Considering personal risk forces us to define personal success. We may well discover that the business failure we avoid and the business success we strive for do not lead us to personal success at all. Most of us have inherited notions of "success" from someone else or have arrived at these notions by facing a seemingly endless line of hurdles extending from grade school through college and into our careers. We constantly judge ourselves against criteria that others have set and rank ourselves against others in their game. Personal goals, on the other hand, leave us on our own, without this habit of useless measurement and comparison.

Only the Whole Life Plan leads to personal success. It has the greatest chance of providing satisfaction and contentment that one can take to the grave, tomorrow. In the Deferred Life Plan there will always be another prize to covet, another distraction, a new hunger to sate. You will forever come up short.

Work hard, work passionately, but apply your most precious asset—time—to what is most meaningful to you. What are you willing to do for the rest of your life? does not mean, literally, what will you do for the rest of your life? That question would be absurd, given the inevitability of change. No, what the question really asks is, if your life were to end suddenly and unexpectedly tomorrow, would you be able to say you've been doing what you truly care about today? What would you be willing to do for the rest of your life? What would it take to do it right now?

On this hilltop I look left toward the Pacific Ocean, across the sloping fields where artichokes and poppies grow, where cattle and horses graze. This is rustic, rancher country. And to the right—all the frantic splendor of the Valley, a teeming maze of highways, bumper-to-bumper traffic, and business parks. Speculators, the Lennys of the world, still keep coming to this small patch of land, this boomtown settlement, and pay astronomical real estate prices for a chance to work their stake. Like the forty-niners 150 years ago, most will leave empty-handed. But some, a few, will amass fortunes and become the leaders of the New. This is a Valley of optimists.

Me, I like being on this ridge, one foot in both camps, one whole from two very different but equally compelling pieces.

In school I belonged to no particular clique, hanging out with a group of people both brilliant and crazy. These peripheral people were highly talented, with off-beat passions, like performing autopsies on busted televisions and computers, building telescopes, practicing ventriloquism, or painting watercolors of dissected animals. Wrapped in their passions, they stood outside the mainstream. I loved their talent and innovation, and I acted like a bridge, connecting them to everything else.

Now I work with inventors, entrepreneurs, and others highly skilled in their own right but not necessarily capable of bringing their ideas to the commercial light of day or achieving the impact their ideas could and should have. This is the creative edge of business—startups, working with a blank canvas to challenge the status quo and make change happen. I work with brilliant entrepreneurs who have a vision for how things can be better and who can't resist doing the next great thing. I am their consigliere.

THE LAST TIME I was in Amsterdam I spent an afternoon in the Rijksmuseum studying the Vermeers and Rembrandts. Rembrandt's *The Night Watch* particularly impressed me. Like many of the Dutch Masters, he painted it on commission for a group of well-heeled patrons. The work portrayed a dozen or so elaborately attired commissioners, reliving the past glory of their civic militia, arrayed according to their financial contribution and status. These were some of the many movers and shakers of Holland's economic Golden Age, affluent and prominent, seeking immortality on canvas. But I was struck that I didn't know any of them, nor did it matter. They were just characters in another man's masterpiece. The only person of importance, the only one whose fame had lasted beyond that period, was the eventually penniless artist—Rembrandt.

Think about *The Night Watch* today, when so many people push and shove with their wealth, fame, and power. In a few hundred years, all of today's movers and shakers may be reduced, at best, to another group of supporting characters on a canvas.

That painting brings to mind a headline from a few years ago: Sam Walton had died the richest man in America, making him, I realized, only the latest in an eternally long line of such record holders. As John Maynard Keynes postulated, in the long run we're all dead.

Time is the only resource that matters.

TO: awhitlock@digger.net
FROM: randy@virtual.net
SUBJECT: Re: One Last Question

I think it's up to you, Allison. If you want to pursue the idea that you and Lenny first discussed, you'll need to take the reins and pull Lenny forward.

You have nothing to lose. Try to answer as many of the questions as you can, but don't worry that you won't have all the answers. Plan how you will discover them.

Good luck.

best

r

Chapter Ten

THE
WHOLE
LIFE PLAN

"WE'RE GOING TO put the fun back into funerals," Lenny said.

Was this my cue? "The fun back into funerals?" I asked.

"Cut it out, Lenny," Allison chided. "I hate that."

Lenny laughed. "I wanted to see your reaction," he admitted. He handed me a copy of his new business plan.

"Besides," he said, "it's more the case now than it ever was."

No denying it. Lenny's sense of humor left a little to be desired, but I was glad to see he was his spunky self again.

"Maybe I should say we're going to put the fun back into Funerals.com," he said. "Except it's not Funerals.com anymore."

Lenny pulled out his extendable pocket pointer, poked at the cover of the plan, and read the title to me: "Presentation to Randy Komisar." Some habits were impossible to break. "Business Plan for Circle-of-Life.com," he continued.

"I can read, Lenny, remember?" I looked at the cover page. "Circle-of-Life. What's that mean?"

"Let's go through the pitch," Allison suggested. "It should all become clear."

"Fine," I said, my curiosity piqued.

It had been ten days since I'd heard from either of them, and I'd assumed the clock had run out. I'd felt sorry that Allison hadn't prevailed and frustrated with Lenny's steadfast denial, but I was also confident the Internet wouldn't lack for casket floggers too long.

Then out of the blue, an e-mail.

TO: randy@virtual.net
FROM: lenny@alchemy.net
SUBJECT: Still Breathing

Randy,

We are not dead yet! After a lot of soul searching in light of all that's happened, we revised the business plan and convinced Frank to give us one more hearing. He'll see us in two days, early afternoon. We'd like to run our ideas by you first. Can we buy your morning chai at the Konditorei?

Thanks,

Lenny

So, here we are again, déjà vu. As usual, the Konditorei had quieted down by midmorning; except for a young couple with a baby in a designer carrier and an occasional take-out customer, we had the sunny place to ourselves. A bootleg tape of the Dead's "Friend of the Devil" played in the background. Connie was kibitzing with the staff, taking a breather. She had welcomed Lenny like an old friend, forgetting for now the putrefying bacteria. She had a natural way with people, and she knew more about business than most of the young bucks who come around here looking for me. I really should discuss a partnership with her.

Lenny's "fun" remark had caught my attention because it was at least the third echo of my first encounter with him, some three weeks earlier. In his corporate uniform again this morning, he had greeted me at the door (without the arm-lock) and guided me to the table where he and Allison had set up shop.

There the similarities, thankfully, ended. Lenny was just as intense, but his energy was leavened with warmth and a sense of humor. Allison, too, seemed to have settled into her own skin, no longer ambivalent or hesitant. She and Lenny were in sync now.

After I sent her my reply, Allison explained, she had spent the weekend strategizing with Lenny. He had been ready to throw in the towel, but she had persuaded him to try another approach.

"So Circle-of-Life.com came out of that weekend?" I asked. They both nodded.

"What we first described to you in Funerals.com," Lenny said, "is still here. But it's only one part of a much bigger idea."

"Does your family all live around here, Randy?" Allison asked.

"No," I replied. "Upstate New York, New England. And my wife's family is from Pennsylvania, Florida, North Carolina. Everywhere but here."

"It's the same with Allison and me," Lenny said. "My family is strong in Boston, but two brothers live in the Midwest, and my sister lives in Florida. My father had seven brothers and sisters, spread all over the East and South, and one out here. Allison's family is scattered around New England and the Southwest."

"In this day and age, families and friends have to work hard to stay in touch. No one writes letters anymore," Allison added.

"When my father died," Lenny explained, "I paid a neighborhood kid who knows HTML to make the site you saw. I wanted a place where the family could gather, post messages, and remember. Not only did it shrink the distance between us, but it made it easier to share feelings. You saw some of the postings. A couple of my aunts and uncles told stories about growing up with Dad, and some of my relatives posted old photographs that we'd never seen before, pictures of Dad as a kid and of the entire family through the years. It was a comfort to all of us to remember Dad and commemorate his life."

"It was a good thing," Lenny went on. "Many of my friends who have visited the site said they'd like to set up a place for their families, too."

"Anyway," Allison chimed in, "when Lenny and I looked at everything fresh we returned to a simple premise. The business should make it possible for people to come together and cope with death and dying. That's our mission."

"And we'll sell caskets," Lenny interjected.

"And we'll sell caskets," Allison concurred. "Absolutely.

That's an expensive decision people have to make at a difficult time. The more information you have, the better the choice."

"Wherever we can find reputable funeral homes who provide good service and take reasonable margins," Lenny said, "we'll work through them. There still needs to be someone local to make the final arrangements. We can steer people to the best facilities and protect them from gouging."

"Not just caskets and liners, but other services too," Allison quickly added. "Counseling, burial sites, gravestones, options for final disposal."

I raised my hand.

"Whoa," I said. "Let's start with the plan." I generally prefer to get off the pat presentation and into the passion, but too much was tumbling out at once for me to absorb.

Lenny and Allison's original idea, the one buried beneath Funerals.com, was to create Internet communities in which family and friends could honor and remember someone who had died. In returning to that idea, Lenny and Allison had expanded it to include people in the process of dying, the terminally ill, and those who care for them.

"We'll make it easy for communities to form around someone's dying and death," Lenny said. "We'll bring together family members and friends, wherever they are in the world, and give them an opportunity to grieve, remember, mourn, and show their support in ways not possible until the Web. At the same time we'll help the dying cope with their own deaths and give them the resources to make plans—financial arrangements and estate planning, for instance—for the families they leave behind. We need to deal with death and dying much better as a society. This business can help."

"We want to make one's last moments as meaningful as possible," Allison continued, "by providing people with the opportunity to connect to those who have given their lives meaning and purpose and, in the end, to make sense of their lives, in an intimate and caring community."

It was about closing the circle of life, I thought.

"This lets us tap into the huge market we talked about before," Allison pointed out, "but in ways much more caring and comprehensive."

"The basic service," Lenny went on, "would be free."

It would include templates and guidelines, he explained, making it easy for anyone to create a community site with photographs and writings. The framework for this basic service would be built with the help of experts in grief counseling and terminal illness, as well as doctors. Those who set up or joined a community could simply visit the site, sign in, and choose from what's available there. Then, if they wished, they could participate more actively by communicating with other members. A simple site would be free, and there would be a charge only if the site exceeded a certain reasonable size or if the activity exceeded a specified time limit, say six months.

Clever, I thought. This way people would be encouraged to use the service for free and pay only when they found it valuable to maintain in the long run. Easy adoption, an Internet version of "trying before buying." Of course, the site would ultimately have to provide real value to convince people to homestead it, but even casual traffic could bring in revenues from advertisers and sponsors.

"Our plan," Allison said, "is to provide targeted information about care, drugs, therapies, and support services for everyone involved in that final stage of life."

Community members wouldn't be bothered by advertising; they would see information on specific services only after they had registered their interest in them. As a result Lenny and Allison wouldn't merely be selling eyeballs, they would be providing qualified leads to their commerce partners. Users could request information and receive answers and referrals to all kinds of resources, some local and some on the Internet. Circle-of-Life.com would charge a fee to merchants in exchange for qualified leads, those people who indicated their interest in finding help. Nonprofits would have free access.

It would be a better arrangement for everyone than simply selling gross demographics to advertisers. Qualified leads were far more valuable to merchants than bulk traffic, and the process would be more consistent with the experience Allison and Lenny wanted to create for community members, less crass and commercial. They also planned to host various events and forums, for which individuals might pay a small participation fee, and which could feature special guest experts or the opportunity to exchange information with members from other related on-line communities that share similar problems or needs. The ability to link separate communities, so members could help each other, would be a particularly useful feature.

For example, they explained, family caregivers, the ones supporting a dying person, often face special burdens, suffering alone in their grief as they continue to care for their loved ones. Circle-of-Life.com would give them a place to communicate with others in similar situations.

"They can turn to each other for support, and especially to express the feelings—their anger, for instance—they can't express to family and friends," Allison said.

Their plan was still to sell the funerary goods they'd identified in the original business. Where there were reputable local sources for those goods, Circle-of-Life.com would refer members to those sources. And where those vendors were commercial businesses, such as funeral homes, Circle-of-Life.com would receive a percentage of the sale, like an affiliate. With this approach, Lenny explained, revenue would come from a larger number of sources.

"One of the weaknesses in the original Funerals.com," I pointed out, "was the issue of finding or being found by those in need. You still have to generate traffic to make this work."

"Yes, of course," Lenny said. "But this approach is more inclusive and less in conflict with the local brick-and-mortar businesses."

He went on to explain that they planned to form alliances with reputable local funeral homes, for which they could be both a source of business through referrals and a Web presence to supplement the funeral home's physical locations. They also planned to form partnerships with those whose daily work brought them in contact with death and dying, including, for example, social workers in hospitals, hospice personnel, and visiting nurses, as well as related membership organizations. They planned to seek endorsements and referrals from national religious organizations of all denominations, which would inform their member churches of the benefits Circle-of-Life.com offered.

In short, their plan was to form a vast web of those whose aims were congruent with their own—to ease the passage of those terminally ill and the grief of the survivors. If they could establish Circle-of-Life.com as the preeminent place to build communities addressing those needs, particularly for far-flung families and friends, that network would provide a competitive advantage. The more people who gravitated to the site, the more valuable it would become to others as they shared information and attracted more local providers of goods and services. Competitors could try to duplicate this model, but once Circle-of-Life.com established itself at the center of the network, competitors would find it difficult to dislodge. This scenario is referred to as the much-coveted "network effect," an increasing return on the benefits of growing scale on the Internet with little or no marginal cost.

What Lenny and Allison proposed to do required an enormous amount of work, and success was far from guaranteed. But here the risk was in the right place—in the execution of the big idea. Their idea embraced fundamental life needs and would employ the proven strengths of the Net, making it hard to believe someone, somewhere, couldn't make it work. If it were to succeed, they would have to execute quickly and with great discipline. They would need to build a vast network of relationships as well. No small challenge.

"Have you made any progress on hiring a team?" I asked.

"We've only had a week or so," Lenny said, "but with our raising some seed money . . ."

"We forgot to tell Randy," Allison said.

Once they had formulated the new idea for Circle-of-Life.com and put together the rudiments of a new business plan, they'd gone back to a small group of angels Lenny had approached months ago. The angels had turned Funerals.com down, but a few were now intrigued enough with the new plan that they had invested $500,000 in seed money.

With that, Lenny and Allison had quit their day jobs to work full-time on the business.

"I thought very hard before turning down that HMO job offer," Allison admitted. "There was a lot I liked about it, the opportunity to build a community of people struggling with serious illness, but once Lenny and I agreed on the basic premise underlying Circle-of-Life.com, I didn't hesitate. This is what I want to accomplish, and if I didn't at least try to do this . . . well, here is my chance. The Internet seems to offer the potential now to do something important in a way never possible before."

I looked through the plan. They had made assumption after assumption about the services offered, sources of revenue, their ability to enter alliances with traditional brick-and-mortar businesses and organizations to form the crucial referral networks, the potential fees and charges. Lenny must have been uncomfortable with those leaps of faith, but the plan also laid out a timetable that identified both the crucial steps and what they hoped and expected to learn at each stage. They were candid and detailed about what they didn't and couldn't know at this point, and they identified how they would refine and reshape the plan as they continued to educate themselves about the market. The plan was a reliable compass, as it should be, not a road map.

They had indeed already made some progress in putting together a team, identifying a strong candidate with a technical background and some startup experience to bring the site up and beginning conversations with a small group of counselors and doctors who were amenable to serving on an advisory board. Someone with accounting experience had expressed interest in joining them part-time in the beginning, expanding to full-time if the thing took off. The team wasn't locked up, but they had apparently found some good candidates who would join as soon as more financing was secured.

They had created simple, pro forma financial statements based on the segments of the existing market they expected to migrate to their service and form the core communities in their network. Then, for each community, they had identified the various potential sources of revenue and the estimated total revenue. It added up to a number that would probably be large enough to get Frank's attention.

"What do you think?" Lenny asked.

Less tidy and tightly wrapped than the Funerals.com presentation, this plan was a bit raw. All in all, though, not a bad job for ten days' work. Most important, the plan communicated a stronger vision, an idea with a wider horizon focused on meeting a critical need. For all its loose ends, it had real potential.

I told them to be completely candid with Frank. Engage him in the power of the idea behind Circle-of-Life.com and enlist him, to the extent he was amenable, in helping them find the answers that would make it a success.

"What if it fails?" I asked. It was a more defensible idea with stronger commercial underpinnings, but it was still a crapshoot.

"We've talked about failure," Lenny said, "and I agree with what Allison said before. I'd always be sorry if I didn't try this. We're realistic about the chances, but we believe we can make this work and grow." He shrugged. "If we do our best and it fails, we'll still be glad we did it. It's worth doing."

"And if it's a great success," Allison added, "this is just the beginning. We'd like to build communities around the entire spectrum of significant life events, like births and graduations and weddings, all the events people want to share with friends and families."

"That's the circle of life in the name," Lenny said. "When we thought about what weaves together all those events, we realized it was the family. People will still be able to build sites for individual events, like a birth or a wedding or a death, but we also want to provide the opportunity for life events to be organized around families. That's the context in which most of those events are celebrated anyway."

"And once you make it easy for family members spread around the world to link up," Allison continued, "you open up a whole new realm. Imagine this—families could connect to form broad and deep genealogies. In a few years our children will be able to go on the Web and surf their way back through generations or jump across a family tree, from the tip of one branch to the tip of another. Rich with pictures and words. Imagine the sense of community that makes possible, even in a world where extended families rarely stay together."

The web of life. The forces of technology pull us apart, and yet that same technology provides the means of staying together.

Lenny smiled. "Most of the advantages of living in a small town with all your relatives," he said, "without living in a small town with all your relatives."

"None of this," he added, "requires new technology. All the pieces exist. What will make Circle-of-Life.com different and attractive is the valuable information we'll provide, the common ground for communication, the simplicity and accessibility of the site, and, ultimately, the communities that will form there."

Lenny looked at his watch and realized they needed to leave for their meeting with Frank.

As they packed their cases, Lenny said, "You must have lots of questions."

"It's a rich idea," I said. "I'll look at the plan in more detail and e-mail you my thoughts."

"Do you think it will work?" he wondered.

"I don't know," I said honestly. "I think somewhere, somehow, something like it will work. As you said, the technology for creating on-line communities exists today. Somebody just has to figure out how to put it together with the right content and information in a compelling way that people will value and someone will pay for."

Allison stood and shook my hand with a satisfied grin.

"Nervous about your meeting?" I asked them.

"Sure," Lenny said. "This is important to us. Frank is doing us a big favor. We can't blow it."

Good, I thought. Welcome to the Whole Life Plan.

"Do you think Frank will like it?" Allison asked.

"I'm not sure," I said. I worried they were seeing Frank a little too early. They had so many ideas that still needed winnowing, refinement, and integration. Focus and organization would be key, as it is in all startups. They would need help strategizing and prioritizing. The good news was they had a wealth of enthusiasm and vision to work with now.

"We're going to make this happen, one way or another," Lenny said. Then he lowered his tone a notch. "Allison and I have talked about it, and we'd really like to have you join us in some fashion. Give it some thought, will you?"

I smiled, flattered as always when someone invites me along for the ride.

I walked with them to their rental. They got in, and Lenny rolled down his window. I leaned over so I could see them both.

"Let me know," I said, "what Frank says. If he's not interested, I might know somebody who is."

Epilogue

THE ROAD

When all is said and done, the journey is the reward. There is nothing else. Reaching the end is, well, the end. If the egg must fall three feet without a crack, simply extend the trip to four.

Nearly twenty-five years ago, stranded on a deserted road in Scotland, this certainty struck me.

It was a damp and dreary day. Cold April rain spit from the steel gray sky. The wind whipped down the hills and ripped right through my winter coat. The landscape was forbidding—craggy, rock strewn, good for a few sheep but not much else.

A friend and I had been on the road for a week or so, hitch-hiking from London. A ride with a long-haul trucker had gotten us to Glasgow, but as we headed east to Aberdeen and then north to Inverness and Loch Ness, friendly drivers, or any cars at all, were harder to come by. Near Aberdeen, we finally landed a ride from a bonny lass, a bit of a talker. She had just broken up with her boyfriend, she admitted, and she seemed intent to practice her flirting. We obliged her and practiced too.

She wasn't going far, so she invited us back to her farm for a bite to eat and a drink. It was clear she meant alcohol, and with my rotten luck—a vegetarian looking for something green to eat in the British Isles—a steaming bowl of haggis.

Hmm. A friendly girl? A little food and a lot of drink? A warm, dry cottage on a cold, wet afternoon? How could I say no?

But my plan simply would not permit it. This place was nowhere, certainly nowhere on my itinerary, and I needed to set my eyes on Loch Ness and hightail it back to London, so I could cross the channel to Paris. I had planned this trip for months, studying the maps and circling the names and places I had to see. I was intent on packing all of Europe's monuments and museums into four or five months, a low-budget, seventies version of the Grand Tour. I had spent years deferring to the exploits of my preppy friends who had already made their tours; I was determined to catch up.

So I dragged my buddy out of the car. On the roadside, the invitation disappearing in the rearview mirror as she drove off, we surveyed our situation: two figures alone on a two-lane road running north-south. I could see in both directions for miles, and there was nothing. No cars. No people. No houses. Only some lonely, dirty sheep, keeping low to stay earthbound in the bluster.

For the first hour or so, we maintained our spirits by joking about our predicament, convinced it would end soon. The few cars that passed paid us no mind, and depression gradually seeped in as we realized there would be no surprises. We could see for miles in both direction, and nobody was coming for us.

As the sky darkened, we left the road and began foraging in the pasture for rocks, optimistically turning back from time to time to scout for our ticket out. A narrow ravine divided the pasture in two, and we started to build stone ducks along the edge. For something to do. To prove we were here. I started tossing stones into the ravine, trying to gauge its depth. Sometimes I could hear the rocks hit the water deep below; sometimes they would bounce off the ravine's steep sides. One, one thousand. Two, one thousand. Three, one thousand. I counted the seconds and tried to calculate the ravine's depth using my best high school physics, but my measurements varied wildly with each throw. I gave up.

Deflated, I sat down in this pasture, head in my hands, trying to figure out how I could reshuffle my painstakingly prepared itinerary to get back on my schedule and salvage this trip. At this rate, it wasn't going to happen. And then, in the middle of my anxious what-iffing, I began to feel a subtle change—the warm touch of the sun on my shoulder. It had succeeded in breaking through the shroud that had enveloped us all day, leaving bright streaks and a burgeoning rainbow. Behind the curtain of mist I finally saw the beauty that had been right before my eyes the entire time—a mad torrent rushing through the sheer ravine, the snaking ribbon of tarmac ahead and behind, and the emerald green hillsides dotted with sheep contentedly munching and chewing. And me, sitting in a quiet pasture on a lonely road in a lost patch of Scotland, in Europe, on an adventure. As the sun burned away the dampness, I realized *this* was it.

With four to five months away from the habits and routines that I had chained myself to at home, this was precious time. What was the sense of rushing down a beaten path with a map I had cribbed from others? This was my trip, my life, and I needed my own journey. I decided to throw away the itinerary and see where this might lead.

More than an hour later, an older couple picked us up and drove us the rest of the way to Loch Ness. We settled in, hung out at the pubs and cafés, took in some of the sites, and savored our time. Eventually, we returned to London. At a party in Soho, I met some people who set me up with their friends in Paris. A week eating bread and cheese, drinking wine from the bottle, and trading off between the *jardins* and the museums—I was ecstatic. Next I met some people grabbing a train to Spain and tagged along. I kept going: Madrid, Lisbon, Morocco, Barcelona, Milan, Venice, Bologna, Florence, Rome, Athens, Santorini, Crete, and everywhere in between. An ever-expanding realm of new characters and experiences greeted me at each stop. A local gadabout in a bar tipped me off to a secluded beach, full of naked travelers, in Corfu. I found it. The border between Greece and Turkey was shut tight over some hotheadedness, but a Swiss girl showed me another route on a fishing boat from Rhodes.

At a crossroads again: Marmaris, Turkey. My Swiss guide was heading for Afghanistan and points east, and she welcomed the company. It was July, getting late, and according to my schedule I should have been heading to Cambridge, Massachusetts, to start another leg of my life. I thought back to the road in Scotland. The choice was all mine. Where was this life headed?

Regrets either way, I forged ahead—to Istanbul. Rumor had it that I could get to Amsterdam from there and that Freddie Laker would honor my ticket to New York. I had never been to Amsterdam. Why not extend my journey another foot?

No time to waste.

ACKNOWLEDGMENTS

A HIGHLY COLLABORATIVE CREATION, this book leaves me heavily indebted to a remarkable group of people: Hollis Heimbouch, my trusty editor and guide, who saw a book where none existed and rolled up her sleeves to make it happen. I am forever hers. Kent Lineback, my partner in crime, who had the unenviable task of trying to form my incoherent ramblings into a story. He worked tirelessly and deserves the credit for much that is right about the book, but he can't be held responsible for its shortcomings. My lovely, precious wife, Debra, who continues to stick by me through thick and thin, even though I give her countless reasons to give up on me. Bill Campbell, my mentor and longtime friend, who refuses to take the blame for anything I may have learned along the way. Bob Roden, lawyer extraordinaire, who shepherded me through the Byzantine business of publishing. Patty Cullen and her merry crew, whose cheery Konditorei makes the best nonfat chai latte in the Valley. Constance Hale, cooler-than-thou, who translated my gibberish into English and got us out of a tight spot. Genoveva Llosa, who was always there with kind and generous support. Dan Kellogg, who put the fun into funerals. The many entrepreneurs, venture capitalists, and other business associates who have given me much more than I can ever return. My dear family, especially my mother, who mercifully avoided any mention in this book, and the innumerable friends, teachers, and fellow travelers I have had the good fortune to meet along the way, all of whom have given me plenty to think about. And, of course, my constant sidekicks, the Horrible Hounds, Tika and Tali, who lounge listlessly at my feet as I toil, rolling on their backs from time to time to demand a rub when they think I may be missing the point.

I thank you one and all from the bottom of my heart.

—Randy Komisar

About the Authors

RANDY KOMISAR lives in Portola Valley, California, with his wife, Debra Dunn, and Tika and Tali, the Horrible Hounds. He currently incubates startups as a Virtual CEO, helping to build businesses from vision and ideas. He has worked as an attorney in private practice and at Apple Computer, as the CEO of LucasArts Entertainment and Crystal Dynamics, as a cofounder of Claris Corporation and CFO of GO Corporation, and as a janitor, baker, and music promoter. He has also helped to build WebTV, TiVo, Mondo Media, and many other emerging companies.

KENT LINEBACK is a writer, producer, and consultant living in Cambridge, Massachusetts. He has produced seventeen film and video programs for Harvard Business School and is currently collaborating on a book about L.L. Bean and completing a screenplay.